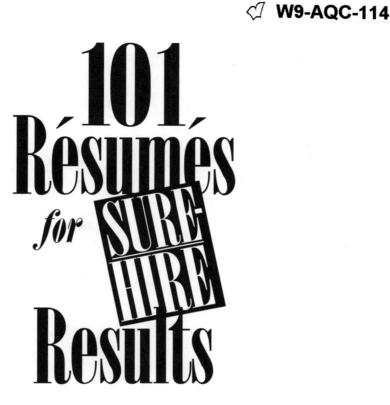

101 Résumés for SURE-HIRE Results

101 Résumés for SURE-HIRE Results

Robbie Miller Kaplan

Author of
Sure-Hire Cover Letters and
The Whole Career Sourcebook

amacom
American Management Association

New York • Atlanta • Boston • Chicago • Kansas City • San Francisco • Washington, D.C.
Brussels • Mexico City • Tokyo • Toronto

This publication is designed to provide accurate and authoritative information in regard to the subject matter covered. It it sold with the
understanding that the publisher is not engaged in rendering legal,
accounting, or other professional service. If legal advice or other expert
assistance is required, the services of a competent professional person
should be sought.

Library of Congress Cataloging-in-Publication Data

Kaplan, Robbie Miller.
    101 résumés for sure-hire results / Robbie Miller Kaplan.
       p.   cm.
    ISBN 0-8144-7871-9
    1. Résumés (Employment)   I. Title.   II. Title: One hundred one
résumés for sure-hire results.
HF5383.K36   1994
808'.06665--dc20   94-6026
                                                         CIP

Printing number

10 9 8 7 6 5 4 3 2 1

Lovingly Dedicated
To my husband, **Jim,**
who makes all things possible,
and to my daughters, **Sam** and **Julie**

Contents

Acknowledgments

I'd like to thank all of my clients who graciously gave me permission to use their résumés.

A big thanks to Jim Kaplan for his computer expertise and willingness to read and critique endless copy.

Thanks also to Mary Fairchild and Betty McManus, for their support and input throughout the project.

And to all of my friends and colleagues who willingly turned over their work histories and résumés.

Introduction

Résumés have never been more important than they are right now. The job market is less secure and more competitive than it has ever been. As companies and organizations continue to "right size," experienced workers are flooding the job market, vying not only with each other but also with recent college graduates for the few positions available.

A lot has changed since I began specializing in résumé creation. Word processing and desktop publishing software have revolutionized résumé production and appearance, making it easier for job seekers to change, target, and modify their résumés.

What hasn't changed is how job seekers avoid, dread, and struggle with writing their résumés. It's understandable: Writing about yourself is difficult. It's a challenge to summarize and articulate your professional life, accomplishments, contributions, and personal uniqueness.

But you *must* have a résumé to look for a job. You need one now and you'll need one for the rest of your working life. Résumés can make or break your ability to secure a job, get promoted, or make a career transition. That's why résumé writing is a skill that is critical to your long-term career success. This book picks up where *Sure-Hire Résumés* left off. It contains dozens of different résumés demonstrating how to translate diverse occupations, qualifications, and experience levels into sure-hire résumés.

Recently, I polled recruiting managers on which résumé characteristics appealed to them—and which turned them off. Although each had his own pet peeves, they all agreed that they looked for résumés that are professional in appearance and readily highlight the qualifications matching their job requirements.

Just think about this: A résumé is one-dimensional, a flat piece of paper. Your goal in writing and producing a winning résumé is to give it depth, to make it come alive by creating a visual presentation of your skills, abilities, qualifications, and experience. Your résumé must become a dynamic introduction to who you are and what you have to offer.

There really isn't a right or wrong way to write a résumé, but there's always a better way. Part One of *101 Résumés for Sure-Hire Results* covers all the basics of résumé writing: whether to use a chronological or functional résumé; how to organize your work history to your best advantage; action words to use when introducing your experience; working with different type styles and design elements (boldface, underlines, upper- and lower-case letters, and choosing the right paper color and weight). Part One concludes with a question-and-answer section based on actual questions my clients have posed to me, covering such issues as:

What do I do if I have worked at only one company?
How do I deal with the fact that I have changed jobs frequently?
How do I present my work experience when I want to make a career change?
What do I do if I only have a high school diploma?
How do I explain a gap of time between jobs?

Part Two is the heart of the book. In it, you'll find 101 résumés representing different career fields and industries. Each résumé is unique in its job seeker's history and qualifications, and in its format, organization, and style. The résumés and experiences are real, taken from job seekers like you; only their names and specific details have been changed to protect the individuals' privacy.

I'd like to suggest that you review all the résumés, not just those that relate to your occupation or field. Use them as a guide for identifying and expressing your individuality, and for creating a résumé that is uniquely you. Spend a few minutes with each one and you'll see how particular words, especially action verbs, are used. Consider how each job seeker's skills and abilities have been presented. Find a format that you like and ask yourself what exactly it is that is pleasing: Is it the typeface? The use of underlines in combination with boldface? The way the information has been set up?

You can do it. Using *101 Résumés for Sure-Hire Results* you can craft a résumé that will get you where you want to go. It's filled with ways you can highlight your strengths, downplay your weaknesses, and present your qualifications dramatically and effectively through words, style, and format.

Part One
Résumé Basics

Simply stated, a résumé is a summary of your qualifications. It includes your education, training, experience, skills, and any additional information that indicates you're a good match for the job you seek.

A résumé is not an autobiography, nor is it meant to present a complete personal or work history. When screening résumés, recruiters and employers are looking for a perfect fit. They're seeking employees whose specific qualifications match their job requirements. They don't have the time to wade through a rundown of experiences and credentials with no relevance to their job requirements.

An effective résumé concisely presents only the qualities that demonstrate your employment capabilities for a specific job. Think of it as a marketing tool that is communicating your experience and abilities. It is a medium that delivers a message about you, determined by what you include in it and how it's presented.

Since employers scan résumés quickly, the first few seconds make a big impression. A résumé that makes a reader slow down and consider it more closely is attractive, concise, and informative.

1
Choose Your Résumé Type

There are two basic types of résumés: chronological and functional. The chronological résumé is the most traditional. It lists your work experience and education in date order, beginning with your most recent and working backwards. Because it will highlight gaps in employment and inconsistencies or frequencies in job moves, the chronological résumé works best for job seekers with progressive and steady work experience.

The functional résumé summarizes experiences and skills in specific areas such as marketing, administration, finance, purchasing, writing, or training. It is used most often to demonstrate transferable skills when moving from one career area to another or to camouflage gaps in employment or frequent job moves. Although you can exclude names of companies and dates, I don't recommend it. Include your work history because employers want to see the positions you've held and where you got your experience.

How should you decide which to use? By determining which one presents your qualifications most effectively. You'll find examples of both in Part Two.

2
Résumé Do's and Don'ts

Do's

1. Do begin with your name, address, and telephone number. You will increase your chances of being reached by including a work number and installing an answering machine on your home telephone. Recruiters will assume that if only one telephone number is listed, it's your home phone.
2. Do include a career or background summary before the main body of the résumé. It's an opportunity to state up front what's special about you.
3. Do strengthen and add authority to your résumé using action verbs. (See the box on page 6 for a selection.) Use a dictionary, synonym dictionary, and thesaurus to expand your choice of words and eliminate redundancies.
4. Do use format and organization to reflect your strengths. If you have been working only for a year or two, begin with your education. If your computer skills are highly desirable, start with them.
5. Do include all relevant honors, awards, and commendations that you have received, as well as certifications and licenses. Highlight any training or professional development courses that have enhanced your skills. List membership and leadership positions in professional associations.
6. Do make sure all of your skills are represented: If you have computer knowledge, are good at writing or public speaking, or can speak a foreign language, get it all down on paper!
7. Do quantify your experience whenever possible. Did you reduce turnover, lower absenteeism, save money, increase customer satisfaction/retention, consistently exceed sales quotas? Clarify what you brought to each experience, describing what you did that was different.
8. Do check your résumé carefully for misspelled words, poor grammar, and syntax. Accuracy is essential.

9. Do use boldface, underlines, bullets, or other special effects for emphasis, and balance all elements with white space. Allow one-inch margins on the top, bottom, and sides of the page. Use full justification and align text in the center for neat margins and evenly spaced text.
10. Do choose quality paper, ideally twenty-four-pound stationery paper with 25 percent rag (good quality) to 100 percent rag (best quality). White, beige, cream, or buff colors are preferable. Produce résumés by photocopying, or by printing originals with a laser printer or letter quality dot-matrix printer.

Don'ts

1. Don't expect an employer to dig through your qualifications. Know the job requirements for the positions you seek and clearly show how you fit them.
2. Don't overlook your special skills (language fluency, familiarity with foreign customs, computer proficiency), your personal attributes (highly skilled in researching and resolving problems with creative solutions), or your career progression (promoted within three months from Editorial Assistant).
3. Don't include personal information such as marital status, number of children, health, height, and weight. Include hobbies and interests only if they add to your credentials, making you a more qualified candidate.
4. Don't overstate your experience, contributions, or accomplishments. Avoid embellishing job titles. Don't lie about degrees or qualifications; it will only hurt you in the long run.
5. Don't include credentials that have no relevance to your job.
6. Don't shift tenses. Current experience should be in the present tense, past experience in the past tense; career objectives, summaries, and personal statements in the present tense.
7. Don't include employer street addresses (use city and state only), names of supervisors, or the reasons you left prior jobs.
8. Don't crowd the résumé with information. One or two pages is acceptable, but more than that should be avoided.
9. Don't use fancy print types or fonts that are hard to read such as calligraphy, Old English, and script. Don't use more than two typefaces together: one for major headings, the other for text and lesser headings.
10. Don't use odd-size or unusually colored paper. Résumés often are photocopied and distributed to others.

For more guidance, consult my book *Sure-Hire Résumés.*

Attention Grabbers - Action Verbs

abstract	create	instruct	promote
achieve	define	integrate	propose
accelerate	delegate	interface	provide
acquire	deliver	interpret	publicize
administer	demonstrate	interview	purchase
advance	design	introduce	raise
advise	determine	invent	recommend
analyze	develop	inventory	reconcile
anticipate	devise	investigate	record
apply	direct	invite	recruit
appoint	distribute	issue	reduce
appraise	diversify	justify	release
arrange	document	launch	represent
assess	draft	lead	research
assign	edit	locate	revise
assist	educate	maintain	route
assume	employ	manage	schedule
assure	encourage	market	screen
audit	enhance	maximize	select
automate	enlarge	mediate	serve
brief	ensure	monitor	set up
budget	establish	motivate	solve
build	evaluate	negotiate	substantiate
chair	execute	obtain	summarize
check	expand	operate	supply
classify	extend	order	support
coach	facilitate	organize	survey
collaborate	formulate	orient	supervise
collect	furnish	originate	teach
communicate	generate	oversee	test
compile	guide	participate	track
complete	head	perform	train
compose	identify	pilot	transcribe
conceive	implement	place	update
conceptualize	improve	plan	utilize
conduct	incorporate	possess	validate
consolidate	increase	prepare	verify
consult	inform	present	write
contribute	initiate	prioritize	
control	inspect	process	
coordinate	install	procure	
counsel	institute	produce	

3
Questions and Answers

Question: The company I've been working with ever since I graduated college just went out of business and I've never written a résumé. Where do I begin?

Answer: The first big step is to reconstruct your work history. Write down on a piece of paper the various job titles you've held and the years in which you held them. List the responsibilities for each job. Ask yourself: What did I accomplish? How did I contribute? Use performance appraisals and letters of commendation to remind yourself of your accomplishments. Also, list your educational background—institutions and dates attended, additional courses or training, special skills and competencies, licenses, certifications, honors or awards, publications, and professional affiliations and leadership positions.

Your résumé must show first, what job or career you are seeking, and second, that you're qualified for the position you seek. Begin the résumé with an introductory statement (see résumé examples 6, 7, 16) or a career summary/history (see résumé examples 28, 30, 42). Build on your strengths, consistently supporting your job qualifications.

Question: Can I include volunteer experiences on my résumé?

Answer: Experience is experience whether it was paid or not. Assess if and how the volunteer work strengthens your credentials. If it enhances your qualifications for the position you seek, include it. I've seen individuals make successful career transitions based on the combination of their volunteer experience, skills, and contributions.

Question: I've changed jobs a lot. Is there a way for me to lessen the negative impact of this?

Answer: Choose a format that will help you downplay dates of employment. For example, you can "bury" the dates by beginning the experience area with job titles in either bold or bold and uppercase typeface. Then, slightly indented on the next line, state the name of the organization, the city, state, and dates of employment, all normal type. Or list your job title flush against the left side of the page and the dates on same line, flush right. For examples, see résumé numbers 4, 8, 30, 49.

Question: I'm a CPA with both corporate and public accounting experience. I'd like to pursue a position in public accounting, but my most recent experience is in the corporate area. Should I use a functional résumé?

Answer: Chronological résumés are required in certain industries, and accounting is one of them. Organize your résumé to bring the most pertinent experience up front. Use two different headings for your experience; begin with "Public Accounting Experience" and follow with "Corporate Accounting Experience." Use a traditional chronological format for the actual experiences, listing the most recent in each area first and working backwards.

Question: I've held professional positions throughout my twenty-year career. I've recently been laid off and need to write a résumé. How do I handle the fact I never went to college?

Answer: You've probably taken many workshops and courses in professional development. Rather than titling a section "Education," opt for "Professional Development." Include a statement that enhances this, such as, "Numerous courses and workshops in management and organization development." Or list the workshops by name and/or the institutions where the programs were conducted. See résumé number 97 as an example.

Question: I completed three years toward a college degree fifteen years ago and have no plans to finish it. Should I just list course work in English in the education section of my résumé?

Answer: You can make this look like an accomplishment by stating in the education section "Completed three years toward a Bachelor of Arts in English."

Question: I recently graduated from college. Since I worked as a painter during summers to pay for my education, I've continued painting while looking for employment. I have some experience in my field of interest, but if I use a chronological résumé, my painting experience would be listed first. Can I list experiences out of sequence?

Answer: Begin your résumé with either a career objective or background summary. Follow with a section called "Related Experience" and include the experience from your field of interest. The next section should be entitled "Summer Experiences." In it, include all of your painting and additional experiences beginning with the most recent and working backwards. See résumé number 5 as an example.

Question: I took a year off from my professional job and worked on my family's farm. How can I fill that gap on my résumé?

Answer: Format the experience just as you would your other experiences. Include the farm name, dates worked, and job title, perhaps Assistant Farm Foreman. Include a description; for example, "Cultivated corn, soybeans, wheat, and tobacco. Maintained apiary of two dozen hives. Provided employee transportation."

Part Two
101 Sure-Hire Résumés

The following résumés are jam-packed with ideas to help you format, organize, and write your own résumé. They are based on the résumés of successful job seekers.

Below you'll find a list that you can use to locate a résumé for a particular career field and/or industry. Also noted are the locations of the functional résumés included, as well as résumés used by career changers and recent college graduates.

Even if you don't see your career or field represented in this list, you can still learn so much by reading each of the résumés. You'll find new ways to express and strengthen your skills, smooth a prior career transition, handle minimal or lack of college education, and turn a varied job history into a positive attribute.

Résumés by Occupation/Industry

Administrative, 4, 35, 60, 77, 101
Computer, 18, 19, 20, 46, 52, 62, 96
Education, 17, 24, 25, 27, 68, 71, 72, 91, 92, 93, 94
Fashion/Retail, 13, 14, 29, 44, 51
Finance, 2, 3, 9, 11, 12, 13, 16, 23, 31, 36, 45, 48, 50, 67, 78
Government, 9, 12, 22, 34, 38, 39, 47, 52, 69, 88
Health Care, 28, 41, 42, 54, 58, 60, 65, 66, 87
Hospitality, 15, 57, 79, 100
Human Resources, 43, 53, 54, 63, 64, 98, 99
Law, 7, 8, 72
Sales/Marketing, 1, 55, 81, 82, 83, 84, 85, 86
Telecommunications, 55, 70, 90, 95, 97

Résumés for Special Cases

Career Change, 19, 30, 40, 42, 44, 48, 54, 61, 62, 80, 86, 89, 90, 98, 99
Functional, 13, 40, 42, 68, 74, 90, 95
Recent College Graduate, 5, 33, 81, 92

RAMONA KENNEDY

7889 Elm Street
Minneapolis, Minnesota 55401
Work (612) 555-XXXX Home (612) 888-XXXX

EXPERIENCED MARKETING AND SALES PROFESSIONAL

WORK HISTORY

ACCOUNT MANAGER

MEDCOM, INC., Minneapolis, Minnesota, 1988 - present

Market, promote, and sell communication systems to the health care industry. Manage a 350+ account base including 10 major hospitals and allied health care centers. Develop regional markets for new products and services. Investigate specific account equipment needs, demonstrate product capabilities, write and present proposals, and negotiate contracts. Maintain an aggressive follow-up, service, and retention program.

Significantly increased regional sales and performance and acquired several new major accounts.

ACHIEVEMENTS

- ◆ Consistently achieve over 100% of sales target.
- ◆ Honored with President's club membership for achieving "Top 5 Percent" nationwide sales standing.
- ◆ Awarded "Salesperson of the Month" four times in 1992.
- ◆ Sales "Rookie of the Year" award.

SALES MANAGER

THOMAS & WOOD, Minneapolis, Minnesota, 1987 - 1988

Managed 9 departments in regional department store. Planned and directed gross profit performance of departments generating $2.5 million in annual sales. Recruited, trained, motivated, and managed a staff of 35 sales professionals. Developed and coordinated sales incentive programs. Maintained inventory control, pricing, merchandising, and sales forecasting.

ACHIEVEMENTS

- ◆ Highest gross profit percentage within 42 stores in the Twin City area.
- ◆ First to implement "Fashion 88," a nationwide fashion merchandising program in conjunction with major modeling studios and local news media.

MARKETING INTERN

UNIVERSITY OF MINNESOTA, Duluth, Minnesota, 1985

Worked on four-month Promotional Lecture Series internship. Developed and implemented a publicity campaign promoting educational lecture series for student body, faculty, and local community. Issued press releases and public service announcements. Conducted surveys and marketing studies for market expansion and public recognition.

EDUCATION

Bachelor of Science in Marketing and Communications, 1986
UNIVERSITY OF MINNESOTA, Duluth, Minnesota

Corporate Training
MEDCOM, INC., "Executive Marketing" and "Sales Training"
THOMAS & WOOD, "Executive Management Training Program"

SHEILAH LOWRY, CPA

99 Willow Lane, Green Bay, Wisconsin 54311
Work (414) 566-XXXX Home (414) 544-XXXX

Career Objective: An accountant in an organization needing expertise in taxes and financial planning.

EXPERIENCE

Senior Tax Specialist, 1990 - present
MCGRADY, MULLENS & ASSOCIATES, Green Bay, Wisconsin

Prepare and review tax returns for corporate and individual clients. Manage the preparation and review of returns for all of the Trust Department customers for First Wisconsin Bank, Green Bay branch.

Interview clients to gather tax information, research tax questions, and advise clients on tax laws. Assist clients with Internal Revenue Service audits. Coordinate and review returns that were prepared through computerized tax service.

Audit and Tax Specialist, 1985 - 1990
DRAKE, SAWYER & ASSOCIATES, Madison, Wisconsin

Performed accounting services for large and small organizations in private industry. Reviewed and prepared tax returns, conducted audits, reviews, and provided litigation support. Developed and conducted training for accounting staff.

Junior Accountant, 1981 - 1985
ARTHUR SHELL & COMPANY, Beverly Hills, California

Prepared clients' personal financial statements, individual tax returns, payroll tax returns, and bank reconciliations for business management firm. Liaisoned with entertainment industry guilds for clients' pension and health contributions.

EDUCATION

Course work toward a **Master of Science in Taxation**
UNIVERSITY OF WISCONSIN-GREEN BAY, Green Bay, Wisconsin

Bachelor of Science in Accounting, 1981
UNIVERSITY OF CALIFORNIA LOS ANGELES, Los Angeles, California

CERTIFICATION

Certified Public Accountant

PROFESSIONAL AFFILIATIONS

American Institute of Certified Public Accountants

MICHELLE HUNTER

7 Pine Lane, Louisville, Kentucky 40225
Work (502) 777-XXXX Home (502) 776-XXXX

CAREER HISTORY

Extensive, progressive experience in corporate accounting with an expertise in evaluating systems and implementing effective, cost-saving procedures.

EXPERIENCE

TECHNICAL SERVICES INC., Louisville, Kentucky

CHIEF ACCOUNTANT, 1988 - present

Manage all accounting functions for technical services firm with $40 million in annual revenue. Coordinate annual audit and local government audits. Perform financial analysis and financial statement preparation for 10 cost centers. Administer 401(k) plan.

Supervise a staff of seven. Delegate, review, and improve accounting procedures; achieve greater productivity and reduce labor costs.

Received the Corporate Achievement Award for sustained and dedicated service.

ACCOUNTANT, 1985 - 1988

Analyzed and reconciled general ledger accounts and prepared entries for accruals on monthly closing. Performed all bank reconciliations. Classified accounts payable, handled vendor inquiries. Examined employee travel expenditures for per diem rates, documentation, and advances. Prepared billings according to contract specifications and collected accounts receivables.

JUNIOR ACCOUNTANT, 1983 - 1985

Processed bi-weekly payroll. Updated changes to the employee database including vacation and sick leave accruals. Validated time sheets and overtime calculations. Prepared quarterly payroll tax returns.

FRY, JONES & DAILEY, Louisville, Kentucky

BOOKKEEPING ASSISTANT, 1982 - 1983

Posted charges to client accounts. Assisted with the implementation of an automated accounting and billing system. Prepared cash disbursements for real estate settlements.

EDUCATION

Bachelor of Science, Accounting, 1984
University of Louisville, Louisville, Kentucky

Associate of Arts, Business Administration, 1982
Jefferson Community College, Louisville, Kentucky

PROFESSIONAL ASSOCIATIONS

National Association of Accountants
American Association of Female Accountants

MELISSA MORGAN

75 Hill Road, Salt Lake City, Utah 84121
Work (801) 521-XXXX Home (801) 421-XXXX

SKILLED ADMINISTRATIVE ASSISTANT

WORK HISTORY

ADMINISTRATIVE ASSISTANT
UNIVERSITY OF UTAH, Salt Lake City, Utah, 1991 - present

Provide administrative support to Provost and staff of 30. Compose, edit, and prepare correspondence. Schedule staff meetings and departmental conferences. Handle travel arrangements including car rental, flight, and hotel reservations. Order and maintain inventory of office supplies.

SENIOR SECRETARY
UTAH STATE UNIVERSITY, Logan, Utah, 1987 - 1991

Handled administrative and secretarial duties for the Chief of Finance. Attended meetings, wrote memos and correspondence, and assisted supervisor in carrying out departmental duties.

SECRETARY
KELLY TEMPORARY SERVICES, Salt Lake City, Utah, 1984 - 1985

Performed administrative support for a variety of firms through temporary placement agency. Long-term assignment with University of Utah.

ADMINISTRATIVE AIDE
WELLS & SWEENEY, ATTORNEYS-AT-LAW, Salt Lake City, Utah, 1981 - 1984

Assisted Administrative Assistant. Answered phones, typed letters and legal documents. Organized files.

MEDICAL SECRETARY
SLC GYNECOLOGISTS, Salt Lake City, Utah, 1978 - 1981

Scheduled appointments and surgery. Completed and submitted insurance documents. Transcribed office notes and letters. Billed patients and collected outstanding accounts.

SKILLS: Proficient with IBM PC, WordPerfect, Lotus 1-2-3; Typing 70 wpm.

EDUCATION

SALT LAKE SCHOOL FOR SECRETARIES, Salt Lake City, Utah
Graduated from two-year program

ROSALIE MILLER
49 Green Avenue, Rochester, New York 14615
(716) 599-XXXX

BACKGROUND SUMMARY

A take charge individual who thrives on challenges and is highly motivated toward achieving goals.

EDUCATION

Bachelor of Science, Business Administration, emphasis Marketing, 1993
University of Rochester, Rochester, New York
Financed 50% of college education through summer employment

SKILLS

Proficient with IBM PC, dBase III+, Lotus 1-2-3, WordPerfect

RELATED EXPERIENCE

ADVERTISING ASSISTANT, Dillon Advertising Agency, Rochester, New York, 1992

Researched and wrote information and services section for organization producing 32 community telephone directories. Conducted sales statistics analysis and prepared reports. Provided input with directory development.

Explored and identified potential advertising clients. Developed marketing strategies and wrote marketing materials.

SUMMER EXPERIENCES

PAINTER, Parker & Hills, Inc., Rochester, New York, 1993, Summers 1988 - 1991

Contracted to supervise workers and paint commercial and residential properties. Progressed to increased responsibility and individual assignments.

SELF-EMPLOYED CONTRACTOR, Rochester, New York, Summer 1987

Partner of a four-member team providing landscaping, painting, and general maintenance to homeowners. Generated business, estimated jobs, scheduled and performed work.

HORTICULTURAL ASSISTANT, West Henrietta Plaza, Rochester, New York, Summer 1986

Maintained inside and outside mall grounds.

JASON HAMMER
88 Broadway, Evanston, Illinois 60201
Work (708) 666-XXXX Home (708) 665-XXXX

Highly skilled architect, licensed in the State of Illinois, with extensive experience in interior design and space planning. Expertise in managing large-scale corporate interior projects.

EXPERIENCE

PRINCIPAL, Jason Hammer Architect, 1991 - current
Founding principal of architecture/interior design firm. Projects include:
> 33 Waco Street Retail Mall Feasibility Study, Chicago, Illinois
> Lesley Miller and Partners, Chicago, Illinois
> Oil America Inc., Chicago, Illinois
> Bill Walters & Partners, Chicago, Illinois
> Child Development Center, Evanston, Illinois
> Franklin Residence, Skokie, Illinois

PARTNER, Bell & York, 1987 - 1991
Managed all interior design activities of the firm's Chicago office. Representative projects included:
> Miller-Smith Offices, Chicago, Illinois
> 89 Main Street Retail Complex, Chicago, Illinois
> South Side Concert Hall, Chicago, Illinois
> Banco Italia, Great Lakes Offices, Chicago, Illinois
> Great Lakes Hotel and Conference Center, Chicago, Illinois
> Rossini Publications Office, Chicago, Illinois
> The Great Lakes Fashion Group, Chicago, Illinois

DIRECTOR OF INTERIORS, White, Wilson, Smith, 1985 - 1987
Handled all interior design projects of the firm's Chicago, Illinois office. Major projects included:
> Smith Hansen & Partners Offices, Chicago, Illinois
> Chicago Union Bank Corporate Offices, Chicago, Illinois

PRINCIPAL, James, Perez & Ross, 1980 - 1985
Managed all interior design projects of the firm's Springfield, Illinois office. Representative projects included:
> Springfield Shopping Mall, Springfield, Illinois
> Springfield Mall Corporate Offices, Springfield, Illinois
> Chicago Union Bank, Springfield, Illinois

PROJECT MANAGER, Kass Shiller Partnership, 1977 - 1980
Managed a variety of large-scale interior design projects.

EDUCATION

CHICAGO STATE UNIVERSITY, Chicago, Illinois
Bachelor of Architecture, 1971, **Bachelor of Science**, 1970

PROFESSIONAL MEMBERSHIPS

American Institute of Architects (AIA) and International Facility Management Association (IFMA)

MARCUS PHILLIP GOODE

65 Birch Street
Birmingham, Alabama 35201
Work (205) 444-XXXX Home (205) 333-XXXX

Experienced attorney with broad general practice background.

ATTORNEY, 1989 - present
Sheldon and Wright, Attorneys-at-Law, Birmingham, Alabama

Render oral and written advice to a variety of clients including conglomerates, universities, and banks. Plan, structure, negotiate, and prepare memoranda, pleadings, briefs, and loan documents.

Represent clients in general contract negotiation and preparation. Ensure clients' compliance with business laws. Advise corporate officers and directors on employment matters and business transactions.

ATTORNEY, 1985 - 1989
Anthony & Hart, Birmingham, Alabama

Drafted manufacturing, licensing, sales, and distribution agreements for new products. Prepared employment and confidentiality agreements and mediated employment contract disputes.

Handled divorces, property settlement agreements, and post-nuptial property agreements. Performed research and wrote motions, briefs, and memoranda on a variety of cases.

LAW CLERK TO HONORABLE BENJAMIN WOOD, 1983 - 1985
Superior Court of Birmingham, Birmingham, Alabama

Wrote memorandum opinions and orders on civil and criminal cases including contract, domestic relations, eminent domain, real property, and misdemeanor.

Served as advisor to Judge on numerous trials and hearings. Trained and supervised seven judicial interns.

JUDICIAL CLERKSHIP

Clerked for Honorable Elizabeth F. Shane, U.S. Court of Appeals (7th Circuit), Mobile, Alabama, 1982 - 1983.

EDUCATION

ALABAMA A&M UNIVERSITY, Normal, Alabama
Juris Doctor, 1982
Bachelor of Arts, 1978

BAR MEMBERSHIPS

Alabama

MARTIN D. SAVAGE

909 Rolling Road
Harrisburg, Pennsylvania 17110
Work (717) 444-XXXX Home (717) 555-XXXX

Career Objective

A position as an attorney specializing in civil litigation.

EXPERIENCE

ATTORNEY
Thomas & Thomas, Harrisburg, Pennsylvania, 1989 - present

Conduct litigation in products liability, personal injury, medical malpractice, and other civil matters. Prepare briefings and pleadings. Handle depositions and discovery. Participate in hearings, oral arguments, and trials in federal and state courts.

ATTORNEY
Peat, Samson, & Shiller, Harrisburg, Pennsylvania, 1985 - 1989

Experienced in criminal and civil litigation; civil jury trials, criminal jury trials, preparation and presentation of appeals before the Supreme Court of Pennsylvania. Civil jury trials included contract disputes, real estate title disputes, and tort. Criminal jury work included felonious assault and murder cases.

ASSISTANT DISTRICT ATTORNEY
Office of the District Attorney, Allegheny County, Pittsburgh, Pennsylvania, 1981 - 1984

Managed intake unit, the case preparation division for Criminal and Supreme Courts. Arraigned 25 to 50 defendants daily in Criminal Court. Argued bail and negotiated case pleas and sentences.

Trained and supervised five junior attorneys.

DEPUTY COUNTY ATTORNEY
Office of the County Attorney, Harrisburg, Pennsylvania, 1978 - 1981

Prepared and tried five to ten cases per month. Wrote and argued motions. Wrote memoranda of law on constitutional and legislative issues. Trained and supervised two junior attorneys.

Increased convictions by 25% by organizing a Federal pilot program, a screening bureau for juvenile delinquency cases.

EDUCATION

PENN STATE UNIVERSITY AT HARRISBURG, Harrisburg, Pennsylvania
J.D., 1981. Graduated in top 10% of class. Associate Editor, Penn Law Review, 1980 - 1981.

BUCKNELL UNIVERSITY, Lewisburg, Pennsylvania
B.A. in English, cum laude, 1978. Dean's List, 4 years.

BAR MEMBERSHIP

Pennsylvania

CHARLES M. HART, CIA
6 Sandy Court, Long Island City, New York 11100
Work (718) 222-XXXX Home (718) 333-XXXX

CAREER OBJECTIVE: A challenging position as an Internal Auditor in private industry.

EXPERIENCE

STAFF AUDITOR
SUFFOLK COUNTY, OFFICE OF INTERNAL AUDIT, Great Neck, New York, 1990 - present

Promoted to Staff Auditor, performing operational, compliance, and financial audits. Use strong analytical and communication skills to develop an expertise in automated information environment. Design audit programs, evaluate internal controls and test results. Develop audit findings, write and edit audit reports.

- Identified additional revenue of $504,000 in most recent audit.

- Received two agency commendations for superior performance, 1991.

Manage in-house technical training program. Use organizational skills to effectively plan long-range training program. Approve training objectives, review work papers, and evaluate presentations.

- Redesigned the in-house technical training program. Designed the audit program for training presentations. Conducted "Train the Trainer" workshop. Incorporated training program revisions into the audit manual.

ACCOUNTING MANAGER
LONG ISLAND SYMPHONY ORCHESTRA, Westbury, New York, 1986 - 1988

Managed accounting function for the organization's annual budget of $850,000. Reorganized and updated accounting operation. Managed computerized accounting system. Handled accounts receivable, accounts payable, and payroll.

EDUCATION

PROFESSIONAL DEVELOPMENT
102 Hours in Continuing Education, Suffolk County and Institute of Internal Auditors
Courses in Accounting, Suffolk County Community College, Great Neck, New York

NEW YORK UNIVERSITY, New York, New York
Master of Arts in Teaching, 1975

CITY COLLEGE OF NEW YORK, New York, New York
Bachelor of Arts, 1972

CERTIFICATION

Certified Internal Auditor (CIA), 1989

ASSOCIATIONS

Institute of Internal Auditors (IIA)
EDP Auditors Association (EDPAA)

PHILLIP GREENE
78 Parkview Terrace
Raleigh, North Carolina 27602
Home (919) 999-XXXX Work (919) 555-XXXX

SUMMARY OF QUALIFICATIONS

Extensive experience in mechanical engineering and expertise in all trades including design, layout, fabrication, hydraulics, heating, air conditioning, electronics, and basic electrical.

EXPERIENCE

SERVICE TECHNICIAN
RMK Ltd., Raleigh, North Carolina, 1990 - present
Foreign Service Center, Winston-Salem, North Carolina, 1986 - 1990

Diagnose problems and repair Porsche and Ferrari automobiles. Ensure customer satisfaction and develop client base.

SERVICE MANAGER
Universal Service Center, Charlotte, North Carolina, 1983 - 1985

Supervised staff and performed service technician responsibilities for Ferrari service division. Implemented inventory control system. Developed client base by planning and operating service clinics. Increased client satisfaction by providing better service. First Ferrari manager to show a profit in organization's ten years in business.

SERVICE TECHNICIAN
Foreign Specialists, Raleigh, North Carolina, 1982 - 1983
International Service Center, Columbia, South Carolina, 1980 - 1982

Handled repairs for imported and domestic automobiles. Developed an expertise with Ferrari automobiles.

EDUCATION

Vocational Institute of Technology, Raleigh, North Carolina, Certificate, 1979

SPECIAL INTERESTS

Repair and restore any make, model, or vintage (domestic or import) automobile.

CERTIFICATIONS

General Certified Mechanic, A.S.E.

ANGELA PETERSON
1411 Tenth Street, Richmond, Virginia 23173
(804) 666-XXXX

BACKGROUND SUMMARY

Twenty-four years of accounting and bookkeeping experience in the areas of accounts payable, bank reconciliations, and personnel records management. Expertise in selecting and utilizing computer systems and software.

EDUCATION

Bachelor of Arts in Business Administration, major in accounting

Rochester Institute of Technology, Rochester, New York, 1967

EXPERIENCE

1982 - present   **Tea Time, Richmond, Virginia**
                                                     Coffee World, Richmond, Virginia

Handle all bookkeeping functions for retail stores located in Monument Mall and State Street Mall. Make daily deposit, balance and audit registers, and prepare monthly closing using Peachtree. Maintain accounts payable program for 600 vendors: review and verify invoices, pay bills, prepare an aging summary, balance 3 checkbooks, and reconcile bank statements. Administer and verify payroll for 15-17 employees. Prepare monthly sales summary and graph for buyers and managers utilizing Lotus 1-2-3. Selected and set up computer system and program.

1973 - 1982   **The Hardware Supply Company, Richmond, Virginia**

Maintained accounts receivable records for 1,500 customers, inventory of 600-700 items, and sales and gross profit records for 12 salesmen using Burroughs L-7 Computer System. Supervised and trained 2 employees to operate computer system. Administered cash receipts and bank deposits, performed analysis and verification of job costing, and audited accounts payable.

1968 - 1973   **Monroe County Health Department, Rochester, New York**

Created, established, and implemented the system for maintaining statistical data for the Monroe County Medicare Program and performed these duties until the Medicare Division was established. Managed four-person office of Accounting Division of Health Department. Prepared and wrote semi-annual Federal and State reports concerning annual financial expenditures. Coordinated Federal Family Planning Project: assisted in formulating program's annual budget request, monitored program's expenditures, and wrote periodic status reports.

1970 - 1973   **Sunshine Day Care Center, Rochester, New York**

Prepared annual budget and financial statements. Organized and administered all cash receipts, cash disbursements, payroll, and accounting functions for a day care center with an enrollment of 80-100.

ELLIOTT GORDON

28 41st Street NW, Washington, D.C. 20016

(202) 812-XXXX

BACKGROUND SUMMARY

Extensive experience in all phases of governmental financial management. Expertise in formulating and executing budget operations.

EXPERIENCE

DEPARTMENT OF NAVY, 1966 - 1993

Senior Budget Analyst, Office of the Chief of Naval Operations

Progressive promotions to positions of increased complexity and scope in all areas of financial management.

Formulated and executed annual budgets of $120 million to support the headquarters staff of the Chief of Naval Operations (senior military official of the Navy). Budgeted for the salaries and fringe benefits of 600 civilian employees plus administrative support for the civilians and 1,200 military personnel.

Budget Formulation
- Prepared written justification, budget exhibits, and backup material to defend budget requests through review staffs within Navy, Office of the Secretary of Defense, Office of Management and Budget, and Congress.
- Coordinated with program officers and superiors; researched and composed responses to review questions.

Budget Execution
- Developed and administered financial plans ensuring sufficient funds were available to pay costs for civilian salaries, travel of military and civilian personnel, office services, vendors, and contractors.
- Obligated funds, monitored expenditures, and analyzed accounting reports to advise superiors on the status of funds.

EDUCATION

B.S., Industrial Administration, American University, Washington, D.C.

Professional Development: Attended numerous courses in financial management and office automation

HONORS/AWARDS

Civilian Meritorious Service Award, 1992

Merit Pay Awards, 1982 through 1992

ALICIA ROLLINS

74 Birchwood Drive
Coral Springs, Florida 33065
Work (305) 888-XXXX Home (305) 333-XXXX

CAREER SUMMARY

Highly qualified retail professional with extensive experience operating a retail specialty chain with three stores in southern Florida.

A proven record of establishing and directing MIS functions. Excellent written and verbal communication skills.

EXPERIENCE

BUSINESS MANAGER, 1992 - present
JJJ Speciality, Coral Springs, Florida

Manage administrative functions and staff for accessory firm. Develop MIS function to meet needs of growing business and implement new accounting software products. Ensure organization provides quality customer service.

Perform all accounting functions. Identify and implement cost-cutting and business improvement measures such as reducing health insurance premiums and telephone expenses.

Made recommendations that resulted in a 50% reduction in outside accounting expenses.

OPERATIONS MANAGER, 1972 - 1992
Sandy Beaches Limited, Miami, Florida

Established a 400 square-foot leather goods retail store in 1972. Developed the business into a 9,500 square-foot, 3-store operation marketing men's and women's clothing, shoes, and accessories. During this period, annual sales grew from $300,000 to $2,000,000.

Managed the evolution of physical and financial operations from manual to computer automated systems, personally conducting the staff training and management. This effort resulted in improved cash flow and increased inventory turnover from three to four times annually.

AREAS OF EXPERTISE

MANAGEMENT INFORMATION SYSTEMS

- Developed and implemented inventory management system and converted from manual to computerized.

- Computer experience includes: IBM PC, DOS, Windows, Unix, Lotus 1-2-3, Excel, Microsoft Word, WordPerfect.

- Computer proficiency in the following accounting software packages: MAS 90, Solomon, AccPac, MAI Basic Four Retail Advantage.

DEVELOPMENT

- Researched demographics and identified potential markets.

- Established business relationships with leasing agents and negotiated lease space and contract terms.

- Selected legal and accounting professionals.

- Negotiated contracts for financing and operating capital to open two stores.

- Coordinated all aspects of opening two new store operations including financing, construction, inventory selection, and store merchandising.

MANAGEMENT

- Managed general operations and office staff including recruiting, training, supervising, counseling, and evaluating performance.

- Supervised all store management in preparing salary and expense budgets and personnel policies.

ACCOUNTING/FINANCE

- Prepared all financial budgets and reports for store operations including daily store register audits, bank reconciliations, and cash disbursements.

- Maintained accounts payable for over 250 merchandise and 100 expense vendors.

- Managed payroll systems for 3 companies, total of 60 employees.

EDUCATION

Miami-Dade Community College, Miami, Florida
Accounting and Business Management courses

CAITLIN TURNER-YORK
1333 SW 79th Street, Miami, Florida 33176
Work (305) 888-XXXX Home (305) 888-XXXX

CAREER HISTORY

Extensive experience buying, managing, and merchandising for large and small multi-store retail operations. Excellent management and interpersonal skills.

EXPERIENCE

BUYER

Atlantic Shoes, Miami, Florida, 1987 - present

Buy and merchandise shoes and accessories for multi-store operation. Supervise staff of 12, coordinate displays, train sales staff on effective selling techniques, and assist in bookkeeping. Maintain inventory using on-line computer system.

BUYER

Macy's, Miami, Florida, 1984 - 1987

Purchased Junior Dresses, Young Junior, and Junior Accessories for 13-store operation. Distributed inventory to maximize sales; initiated, recommended, and coordinated advertising. Prepared fashion forecasts and trends and conducted sales training.

BUYER

Jordan Marsh, Miami, Florida, 1977 - 1984

Progressive promotions to Buyer of Young Junior Sportswear and Dresses. Handled all phases of buying and merchandising for nine-store operation.

ASSISTANT BUYER

McCurdy's, Rochester, New York, 1974 - 1977

Coordinated all merchandise for Women's Sportswear department. Received, ticketed, and transferred merchandise. Recorded, updated, and reported on department sales.

EDUCATION

B. S., Merchandising, Rochester Institute of Technology, Rochester, New York, 1974

FELICIA BACON

75 Magnolia Street, New Orleans, Louisiana 70115
Work (804) 888-XXXX Home (804) 222-XXXX

Career Objective: A catering management position in a large hotel or conference center.

EXPERIENCE

MARRIOTT HOTEL, New Orleans, Louisiana
Catering/Conference Manager, 1990 - present

Coordinate large conferences in luxury hotel. Develop relationships with corporations and non-profit organizations and build referral business. Prepare budgets, plan and supervise conferences. Create menus, organize all food and services, and follow up to ensure client satisfaction. Acting Director of Catering/Conference Management in Director's absence.

CAJUN SEAFOOD, New Orleans, Louisiana
Director of Sales and Catering, 1988 - 1990

Developed and organized sales and catering department in new upscale restaurant. Created marketing strategies, developed menus, organized and managed private events. Hired and trained staff. Performed accounting functions during Vice President of Finance's absence.

HOTEL REGENCY, Baton Rouge, Louisiana
Restaurant Manager, 1985 - 1988

Promoted from Morning Manager. Operated hotel's Food and Beverage Department. Developed entire service system. Hired, trained, and supervised 2 floor managers, 3 departments, and a staff of 35. Established wine and liquor procedures. Prepared forecasts and budgets.

ALLEGHENY MANAGEMENT DEVELOPMENT CENTER, Pittsburgh, Pennsylvania
Conference Service Manager, 1982 - 1985

Organized new service system for large conference center. Designed special event programs and coordinated conference service functions. Hired, trained, and scheduled staff of 20. Assisted General Manager with special projects.

EDUCATION

UNIVERSITY OF PITTSBURGH, Pittsburgh, Pennsylvania
Bachelor of Business Administration, 1982
Internships at Hyatt Hotel, Pittsburgh, Pennsylvania and Liberty Hotel, Philadelphia, Pennsylvania.
Dean's List, two semesters.

SKILLS

Proficient with IBM PC, Lotus 1-2-3, and WordPerfect

REGINA BAKER
9 Pebble Beach Road, Tampa, Florida 33600
Work (813) 222-XXXX Home (813) 223-XXXX

FINANCIAL MANAGEMENT PROFESSIONAL

EXPERIENCE

CHIEF FINANCIAL OFFICER/EXECUTIVE VICE PRESIDENT
Tampa Bay Health Products, Tampa, Florida, 1992 - 1993

Set up joint venture accounting and strategic planning departments for health product distributor. Raised money through public limited partnerships. Served as part of the 4-person team that negotiated 75 page prospectus with Merrill Lynch. Conducted presentations at brokerage houses and raised $3.5 million.

CHIEF FINANCIAL OFFICER
Raleigh Construction Company, Tampa, Florida, 1985 - 1991

Provided overall guidance and direction of finance and accounting functions for both the mechanical contracting and real estate divisions of an organization with approximately $20 million in annual revenue. Hired, supervised, guided, and evaluated staff of 7.

Created all financial documents and established purchase order system. Developed cost control program for use in evaluating job costs.

Implemented computerized payroll, accounts payable, accounts receivable, and general ledger functions.

CHIEF ACCOUNTANT
Coastal Construction, Palm Beach, Florida, 1977 - 1984

Reviewed separate company financial statements and federal and state income tax reports for seven subsidiary companies and prepared consolidated summaries. Selected and monitored corporate insurance. Supervised a staff of six.

CHIEF ACCOUNTANT
Sun Enterprises (Subsidiary of Coastal Construction), Boca Raton, Florida, 1968 - 1977

Assisted in selecting and implementing modern computer technology and systems and establishing new corporations as company grew from local general contractor to one of the largest general contractors in the state of Florida.

Supervised and administered accounting department. Prepared internal financial statements and state and federal income tax reports. Selected and monitored insurance program.

ASSISTANT CONTROLLER
ADH Electric Company, Inc., Miami, Florida, 1966 - 1968

Progressive advancement from Accountant to Assistant Controller.

CHIEF COST ACCOUNTANT
CG Electric Company, Coral Gables, Florida, 1961 - 1966

Progressive advancement from Internal Auditor to Chief Cost Accountant.

EDUCATION

B.S., Accounting and Economics, University of Florida, Gainesville, Florida

ROSS ANTHONY
18 Laurel Lane, Columbus, Ohio 43210
Work (614) 777-XXXX Home (614) 766-XXXX

Experienced College Administrator

EDUCATION

UNIVERSITY OF CINCINNATI, Cincinnati, Ohio, **Ph.D., major, Higher Education, minor, Counseling**, 1984;
M.A., major, History, specializing in Latin America, 1976

UNIVERSITY OF OREGON, Eugene, Oregon, **B.A., major, History, minor, English**, 1974

EXPERIENCE

OHIO STATE UNIVERSITY, Columbus, Ohio
DIRECTOR OF COLLEGE ACTIVITIES, 1980 - 1981, 1984 - present

Work with students, faculty, staff, and alumni to create and provide a well-balanced educational, social, recreational, and cultural experience for members of the college community. Teach an undergraduate course, "College Union Management and Programming," and supervise independent study course for seniors interested in research in higher education.

Collaborate with Student Affairs staff in developmental workshops and supervise the academic and social summer programs for new students. Manage a professional and support staff of nine.

SELECTED ACCOMPLISHMENTS

- Coordinated ten session program, "Your Future in Retirement," open to the community.
- Created an Issues and Answers Program for students, faculty, administrators, and the community. Topics included Human Sexuality, The Role of the Faculty in the Classroom, The Role of Faculty in Academic Advisement, and The Language Requirement.
- Initiated bi-weekly call-in radio show, "On the Line," highlighting different groups and issues.
- Introduced *Capsule*, weekly newspaper, to serve as continuing orientation program for freshmen.
- Implemented a paid Student Internship in Activities and College Unions for undergraduates desiring student personnel as a profession.
- Served as advisor to the Student Association, Board of Governors, International Club, Yearbook, Campus Radio Station, Inter-Sorority Council, Lecture Board, and Lyceum.

UNIVERSITY OF CINCINNATI, Cincinnati, Ohio
GRADUATE ASSISTANT, STUDENT AFFAIRS, 1982 - 1983

Established first Professor/Course Evaluation Book and weekly international student/faculty luncheons.

GEORGE WASHINGTON HIGH SCHOOL, Cleveland, Ohio
HIGH SCHOOL TEACHER, 1976 - 1977

Taught history to grades 9 and 10.

PROFESSIONAL ASSOCIATIONS

National Association of Student Personnel Administrators

PETER W. OWENS

8 Ridge Road
Gaithersburg, Maryland 20878
Work (301) 988-XXXX Home (301) 998-XXXX

Extensive progressive computer experience with both hardware and software. Technical expertise and excellent problem-solving skills.

EXPERIENCE

RKK Corporation, Bethesda, Maryland, 1970 - present

REGIONAL INSTALLATION MANAGER, 1988 - present

Plan, coordinate, and monitor installations of large-scale computer systems for U.S. Government installations worldwide. Act as interface between customers and RKK Corporation. Provide whatever resources are necessary and ensure a successful and timely installation.

Designed a PC-based dispatch and call-tracker system for the Federal Computer System (FCS) accounts in Europe. Set up a local area network (LAN) project at the Bethesda, Maryland facility.

TECHNICAL MANAGER, 1985 - 1988

Monitored technical problems and found solutions for overseas U.S. Government accounts. Identified failure patterns and recommended solutions.

ENGINEER IN CHARGE, 1975 - 1985

Maintained 4 large-scale systems for the Department of Defense. Worked closely with customer to ensure equipment satisfaction and provided 24-hour technical support. Supervised staff of 6 and assigned and monitored work responsibilities.

TECHNICAL REPRESENTATIVE, 1970 - 1975

Provided support for computers installed in suburban Maryland. Promoted to Group Leader. Supervised staff of 30.

PROFESSIONAL TRAINING

Extensive training in repairing large-scale hardware.

Willing to Relocate

REYNOLDS W. STACK

49 Highland Road, Hartford, Connecticut 06105

(203) 999-XXXX

Career Objective: A computer programmer or analyst position.

EDUCATION

UNIVERSITY OF HARTFORD, Hartford, Connecticut
Anticipate **Bachelor of Science in Computer Information Systems,** March 1994
Current GPA 3.9; Dean's List
Diploma Program in Computer Information Systems, 1993

TECHNICAL SKILLS

SOFTWARE: RMCOBOL 85, C, C++, dBASE III+, BASIC, QBASIC, Pascal, WordPerfect, Lotus 1-2-3

OPERATING SYSTEMS: MS DOS 5.0, UNIX

EXPERIENCE with systems analysis and design; modular programming, integrated database systems, array processing and table handling; file maintenance including sequential, sorting and merging, indexing, interactive processing; pointers, structures, and bitwise operations. Proficient in technical writing.

BACKGROUND SUMMARY

Expertise in operating, repairing, and maintaining mechanical equipment. Comprehensive background in diesel engine mechanics. Qualified Quality Assurance Inspector and Navy SCUBA Diver.

Consistently received the highest performance evaluations, recipient of numerous Letters of Commendation and nominated **Sailor of the Quarter** for sustained superior performance.

"Petty Officer Stack is a top performer who is head and shoulders above his contemporaries...A highly qualified technician in any endeavor, no task eludes his keen and professional abilities." Commanding Officer, USS DOLPHIN, 4/23/90

EXPERIENCE

UNITED STATES NAVY, USS DOLPHIN, 1985 to 1990

Machinist's Mate Second Class Petty Officer
Submarine Qualified

Supervised 15 watchstanders and technicians in the performance of maintenance, troubleshooting, and repair of all shipboard high-pressure air systems, chilled water systems, atmosphere control systems, hydraulic systems, sanitary systems, trim and drain systems, and miscellaneous pumps and valves. Operated and performed corrective and preventive maintenance on the ship's Electrolytic Oxygen Generator. Cited for supervising the successful overhaul of ship's high-pressure air compressors during an abbreviated upkeep, significantly upgrading their reliability. Provided formal and on-the-job training on the operation and maintenance of auxiliary mechanical systems.

Designated and certified a Navy Quality Assurance Inspector. Performed inspection and test (stop, in-process, and final) of all auxiliary, mechanical, and ship control systems. Wrote work requirement and procedure packages.

Supervised and conducted all underwater repair and maintenance requirements. Trained new divers and checked all equipment.

ALEXANDER BUTLER

88 Ashford Lane, Detroit, Michigan 48226
(313) 888-XXXX

Progressively responsible experience in computer analysis and programming.

SKILLS

HARDWARE: IBM mainframe OS/MVS/XA, JCL, utilities
SOFTWARE: IMS, TSO/ISPF, COBOL, Panvalet, DB2/CICS

SENIOR PROGRAMMER/ANALYST
Great Lakes Airlines, Detroit, Michigan, 1988 - present

Analyze, design, and implement application software systems; handle project coordination, user interface, system design, programming specifications, task scheduling, program testing, implementing, and documentation. Projects include marketing, general accounting, ticket refunds, and travel agency sales.

Designed and installed a new travel agency revenue based system with 50 COBOL programs. Maintained and enhanced the database as on-going project. Provided a series of special reports to research a potential security/fraud situation.

PROGRAMMER/ANALYST
Great Lakes Transit, Detroit, Michigan, 1985 - 1987

Developed and maintained payroll systems; designed and implemented a retroactive pay system for union employees.

PROGRAMMER/ANALYST
University of Michigan, Ann Arbor, Michigan, 1983 - 1985

Researched and developed a statistical reporting system for minority groups.

PROGRAMMER/ANALYST
Bank of Ann Arbor, Ann Arbor, Michigan, 1980 - 1983

Developed accounting systems utilizing structured programming techniques in an R&D environment.

PROGRAMMER
Michigan Department of Education, Grand Rapids, Michigan, 1978 - 1980

Enhanced programming skills by coding, debugging, and testing programs.

EDUCATION

Bachelor of Science, Business Administration, 1978
University of Michigan, Ann Arbor, Michigan

WILLIAM H. WOOD
88 Mountain Avenue, Ontario, California 91760
(714) 888-XXXX

CAREER SUMMARY

Experienced **contracts professional** with strong communication skills and working knowledge of FAR/DAR, contract/legal issues. Expertise with all types of contracts.

EXPERIENCE

THE AEROSPACE COMPANY, Los Angeles, California

SUPERVISOR, CONTRACT ADMINISTRATION, 1991 - present

Supervise the ongoing administration of all division contracts delivering sophisticated guidance systems and support services to government, commercial, and international customers for defense applications. Supervise staff of four.

Established and directed team to review requests for proposal, assess business and technical risk, formulate and recommend bid strategy to management, and support proposal effort.

SENIOR CONTRACT ADMINISTRATOR, 1986 - 1991

Administered increasingly complex production and development contracts including the co-production of a major system in Europe.

Successfully negotiated large multi-year production contract and administered a fixed price development contract.

CONTRACT ADMINISTRATOR, 1983 - 1985

Handled all aspects of the administration of production contracts with government and commercial customers including review of requirements through proposal preparation, negotiation of price and terms, and contract compliance monitoring.

NATIONAL ASSOCIATION OF STATES, Washington, D.C.

ASSISTANT TO THE EXECUTIVE DIRECTOR FOR FEDERAL PROGRAMS, 1980 - 1983

Maintained liaison with federal agencies, Congress, and public interest groups concerned with mental health issues on behalf of state directors. Convened annual meetings and published monthly newsletter for state funding directors.

EDUCATION

M.B.A., Finance, 1991, University of California, Irvine, Irvine, California

B.A., Psychology, 1979, Pepperdine University, Malibu, California

Professional Development
Numerous courses in financial management, negotiations, FAR/DAR, and contract types
Computer training in Paradox and Lotus 1-2-3

PROFESSIONAL ASSOCIATIONS

National Contract Management Association

ROLAND T. NELSON

32 Dupont Circle
Washington, D.C. 20001
Work (202) 444-XXXX Home (202) 888-XXXX

BACKGROUND SUMMARY

Extensive experience in all phases of contracting from initiation to completion. Expertise in negotiation procedures, contract preparation, pricing, government regulations, and oral presentations. Strong interpersonal, writing, and organizational skills.

EXPERIENCE

CONTRACT SPECIALIST
DEPARTMENT OF TRANSPORTATION, Washington, D.C., 1978 - present

Process all acquisition actions from initial preparation/solicitation through negotiation, approval, award, and administration. Individual procurements are apportioned approximately equally between cost-reimbursement type and fixed-price type; are both competitive and noncompetitive; range from approximately $100,000 to $130 million in value; and may be either fully "open market" or minority contract set asides. Major participant in contract efforts supporting National Airspace System (NAS) Plan and Rotorcraft Master Plan implementation, and establishment of airport passenger security systems.

Maintain contact with requirements/technical, program management, legal, pricing, and budget personnel in-house as well as with contractors. Participate in pre-acquisition planning.

Handle all modifications and administration of assigned programs/contracts from initiation to completion. Prepare all supporting documentation for contract award and administration.

CONTRACT SPECIALIST
DEPARTMENT OF ENERGY, Washington, D.C., 1975 - 1978
DEPARTMENT OF THE INTERIOR, Washington, D.C., 1974 - 1975

Conducted technical coordination, procurement planning, solicitation, proposal evaluation, cost analysis, negotiation, and award of contracts. Administered and modified contracts after award. Contracts placed with commercial R&D firms, universities, and research institutions with values of approximately $250,000 to $10 million.

Assisted in contract policy development, contract format development, acquisition scheduling, budget development, management status briefings, and personnel appraisals.

CONTRACT SPECIALIST

U.S. Army Mobility Equipment Research and Development Center, Fort Belvoir, Virginia, 1962 - 1974

Planned, justified, solicited, evaluated, negotiated, awarded, and administered major procurements (mainly R&D-oriented) in countermine/counter intrusion sciences, electrical/electrochemical night warfare systems/devices, fuels research, water decontamination, heating and air-conditioning, major multi-purpose vehicles, and containerization. Contracts ranged in value from approximately $50,000 to $30 million, approximately 70% cost-reimbursement type and 30% fixed price.

Largest programs included the implementation of computerized logistics and personnel administration under the Automated Data Systems for the Army in the Field (ADSAF) concept and a Vietnam-era 3-service support project for seismic sensor development (classified SECRET).

Supervised three contract specialists and one clerical. Promoted from lower grade specialist position to contract specialist.

EDUCATION

UNIVERSITY OF PITTSBURGH, Pittsburgh, Pennsylvania
B.B.A. in Industrial Management, 1959
PROFESSIONAL DEVELOPMENT
Over 18 courses/workshops/seminars on the topics of Acquisition Management, Contract Law, Incentive Contracts, Pricing, and related subjects

HONORS/AWARDS

Outstanding Performance rating - 1989

Exceptional Performance ratings - 1987, 1990

MILITARY SERVICE

U.S. Army active/reserve (enlisted) - December 1960 to October 1966

ALEXANDRA TOMLINSON, CPA
78 Victoria Road
Cincinnati, Ohio 45227
Work (513) 333-XXXX Home (513) 888-XXXX

CAREER SUMMARY

Extensive experience in all aspects of developing, implementing, and administering accounting and tax functions for a wide range of organizations.

CORPORATE ACCOUNTING EXPERIENCE

CONTROLLER
Worldnet Corporation, 1988 - 1993

Accounting and administrative responsibility for a vertically integrated organization with sales of $75 million. Prepared budgets and financial statements, analyzed payables and receivables, and implemented credit and collection programs.

Prepared and audited employee and sub-contractor payroll, state sales taxes, and bank reconciliations. Planned and controlled physical inventory and year-end audit.

Organized, directed, and controlled the work of accounting personnel in collecting, summarizing, and interpreting data for management, creditors, investors, and tax authorities. Developed forecasts for proposed expansion projects. Created reports for management by measuring actual performance against operating plans and standards.

ACCOUNTING OPERATIONS MANAGER
International Carpets Inc., 1975 - 1981

Managed financial operations for the textile division. Handled accounts receivable, billing, accounts payable, payroll, sales tax reporting, and inventory control. Managed a staff of 30.

Designed and implemented a fully integrated accounting system. Improved accuracy of billing and accounts receivable.

Updated the accounting and operations procedures manual and improved travel and entertainment reporting.

ASSISTANT CONTROLLER
Allied Industries, 1971 - 1973

Supervised collection and interpretation of accounting data. Oversaw statutory and management reporting functions. Prepared detailed journal entries and account analyses. Assisted in preparing financial statements.

PUBLIC ACCOUNTING EXPERIENCE

PARTNER
Barth, Little, Tomlinson, CPAs, 1984 - 1988

Provided full range of accounting services for clients from individuals to large commercial organizations. Participated in all business aspects of operating a professional services firm.

SOLE PRACTITIONER
Alexandra Tomlinson, CPA, 1981 - 1984

Built a certified public accounting practice specializing in small- to medium-size businesses. Performed full range of accounting services.

TAX MANAGER
Williams & Thomas CPAs, 1973 - 1975

Provided accounting services for large and small organizations in private industry. Performed tax planning, reviewed and prepared tax returns. Specialized in researching unusual tax matters.

STAFF ACCOUNTANT
Henry James CPA, 1970 - 1971

Acquired accounting, income tax, and auditing experience.

EDUCATION

OHIO WESLEYAN UNIVERSITY, Delaware, Ohio
M.S.A., 1972
B.S., Accounting, 1970

CERTIFICATION

Certified Public Accountant

PROFESSIONAL AFFILIATIONS

American Institute of CPAs
Ohio Association of CPAs

MARILYN GILLEN

15 Coastal Highway   Seattle, Washington 98121
Work (206) 999-XXXX   Home (206) 888-XXXX

CAREER SUMMARY

Experienced counselor in higher education with expertise in the fields of career/life planning, professional development, and community college education.

EDUCATION

Ed.D., 1993, University of Seattle, Seattle, Washington. Counselor Education with cognate area in Higher Education Administration. Awarded graduate assistantship as Coordinator of Personal & Career Development Center in the School of Education. Dissertation assessed the professional development needs of community college counselors in Washington.

M.S., 1973, Gonzaga University, Spokane, Washington. Concentration in Personnel Services and Counseling. Awarded a graduate assistantship as Assistant Director of Placement for the University.

B.A., 1971, Walla Walla College, College Place, Washington. Major in Social Science and Psychology.

PROFESSIONAL EXPERIENCE

Associate Professor/Coordinator of Off-Campus Counseling Programs
SOUTH SEATTLE COMMUNITY COLLEGE (SSCC), Seattle, Washington, 1976 - present

Administer off-campus services for military personnel at Fort Henry and Headquarters, U.S. Navy. Provide counseling and other student support. Supervise SSCC staff responsible for admission and records, student payments, military tuition assistance, and publicity. Coordinate 40 course offerings for 800+ students per semester and other SSCC activities with military education centers.

Coordinate career and life planning programs. Provide academic, career, and personal counseling to students and community members in groups and individual sessions.

Develop and teach three-credit psychology course to facilitate career and life planning processes.

Selected Accomplishments

Professional Development

♦ Designed a system for equitable disbursement of human resource development funds totaling $40,000 as chair of faculty HRD committee. 1991 - 1992.

♦ Appointed to the Chancellor's Professional Development Task Force to design a faculty professional development program for the Seattle Community College Symposium. 1992 - 1993.

♦ Wrote proposals regarding disbursement of faculty tuition assistance and interview policy as chair of campus faculty professional development committee. 1992 - 1993.

Career/Life Planning

♦ Co-authored *Career Directions: A Guide for Career/Life Planning* (4th edition) published by Smith-Hart, written to facilitate the career/life development of the adult student. This text is used throughout the United States and Canada.

♦ Designed and implemented a comprehensive career and life planning service for students, faculty, and the community including job fairs, workshops, classes, and counseling. Trained counselors and interns to facilitate classes and workshops. 1976 - present.

♦ Obtained 3 grants totaling $25,000 to evaluate effectiveness of the counseling services, write career/life materials for adults, and link community resources with the community college. 1980, 1982, 1987.

♦ Presented and consulted at local and national professional conferences in the community and colleges on topics including Team Building Using the MBTI, Increasing Self-Esteem, Career Development for the 21st Century, and Adult Life Transitions. 1976 - present.

RELATED EXPERIENCE

Director of Student Affairs, Seattle University, Seattle, Washington, 1974 - 1976
Assistant Director for Placement, Gonzaga University, Spokane, Washington, 1973
Admission Counselor, Walla Walla College, College Place, Washington, 1971 - 1973

PROFESSIONAL CERTIFICATIONS

National Certified Counselor (N.C.C.)

National Career Counseling Certification (N.C.C.C.) from National Board of Certified Counselors, an affiliate of the American Counseling Association

PROFESSIONAL AFFILIATIONS

American Counseling Association
Washington Community College Association
Washington Counselor Association
Washington College Placement Association

ALLEN GRIFFIN
50 Plantation Lane
Atlanta, Georgia 30341
(404) 888-XXXX (work) (404) 555-XXXX (home)

BACKGROUND SUMMARY

Fourteen years of higher education counseling with a specialty in establishing effective programs to prepare, guide, and develop students.

EDUCATION

Education Specialist, Human Resource Development, 1989
   Emory University, Atlanta, Georgia

Master of Science in Education, College Student Personnel, 1982
Bachelor of Music, Music Education, cum laude, 1979
   University of Miami, Coral Gables, Florida

EXPERIENCE

Southern Georgia Community College, Americus, Georgia

COUNSELOR/ASSISTANT PROFESSOR, 1988 - present

Initiate and implement all recruitment efforts for college campus of 4,000 students. Prepare and make presentations at local high schools and attend college fairs. Advise and direct students on college majors, course selection, and career planning.

- Create and teach a variety of career development courses and workshops including "Leadership Skills for Women," "Employee Interviewing Skills," "Resume Writing," and "Job Search Strategies."

- Selected as one of two campus faculty for "Project International Emphasis." Promote international and multicultural awareness through workshops, internal communications, and meetings.

- Successfully chaired collegewide annual Student Leadership Award Banquet. Increased student participation and effectively managed program for five campuses.

- Managed $24,000 student activities budget.

George Washington University, Washington, D.C.

ASSISTANT DIRECTOR OF STUDENT ACTIVITIES, 1985 - 1988

Designed and coordinated all undergraduate orientation programs for campus of 6,000 students and leadership programs for 200 campus organizations. Developed and presented workshops on "Management and Leadership," "Participatory Management," and "Motivating Volunteers."

- Contributed innovative design and improvements to all orientation materials including *Student Handbook, Orientation Schedules, Foggy Bottom Area Banking, Getting Started* and *District Hot Spots.*

- Increased and diversified participation and attendance at numerous leadership conferences and activities.

Emory University, Atlanta, Georgia

RESIDENT DIRECTOR, 1982 - 1985

Managed staff of 12. Interviewed, hired, trained, evaluated performance, and counseled. Chaired committee to interview, select, hire, and train 50 Resident Assistants.

- Supervised residence hall operations for 500 students. Direct responsibility for budgets, student services, conflict resolution, and building maintenance.

University of Miami, Coral Gables, Florida

ASSISTANT COMPLEX DIRECTOR, 1980 - 1982

Served on management team with rotating responsibilities for residence hall with 1,400 students. Supervised 13 Resident Assistants, provided staff development, and served on numerous committees for staff selection, funding allocations, and training. Managed $10,000 programming budget.

INTERN AND VOLUNTEER, 1977 - 1982

Surveyed students, planned programs, and taught a variety of workshops and seminars including "Leadership Training Program" and "Human Potential Seminar."

PROFESSIONAL MEMBERSHIPS

Georgia College Personnel Association, Past President

American Society for Training and Development

American College Personnel Association

BRANDON MURPHY
34 Dogwood Lane, St. Louis, Missouri 63117
Work (314) 777-XXXX Home (314) 999-XXXX

EXPERIENCED CUSTOMER SERVICE MANAGER

WORK HISTORY

AMALGAMATED INDUSTRIES, St. Louis, Missouri

CUSTOMER SERVICE MANAGER, 1991 - present

Develop and implement credit and collection programs and maintain cash flows for $75 million in annual revenue. Ensure the validity of customer billings and administer customer care programs. Manage a staff of 10; recruit, supervise, develop position descriptions; establish performance criteria and appraise performance.

Consistently exceed all credit and collection targets and achieve a days sales outstanding of 28 days.

DISTRICT BILLING MANAGER, 1988 - 1991

Managed billing department for 5 branch offices with a machine population of 16,000 units and annual revenue of $66 million. Direct responsibility for staff of 8. Effectively trained staff resulting in highest billed population in district. Promptly handled customer inquiries and efficiently resolved billing problems.

MAJOR ACCOUNT ADMINISTRATOR, 1984 - 1987

Coordinated and implemented a new major account price plan. Developed procedures, initiated changes in corporate policy. Created and conducted presentations on contractual terms and issues to customers, sales, and administration.

QUALITY MANUFACTURERS, St. Louis, Missouri

CREDIT MANAGER, 1982 - 1984

Managed credit department for automobile accessory manufacturer. Approved credit, resolved billing and credit problems, and collected outstanding receivables. Supervised staff of one.

CREDIT REPRESENTATIVE, 1978 - 1981

Initiated collection programs for delinquent accounts. Identified billing and collection problems and followed through to resolution. Developed expertise in credit and collection procedures.

EDUCATION

Associate in Arts, Liberal Arts, Maple Woods Community College, Kansas City, Missouri, 1977

PATRICE HORRIGAN
85 Heather Place
Burlington, Vermont 05402
Work (802) 333-XXXX Home (802) 444-XXXX

BACKGROUND SUMMARY

Dedicated and experienced educator specializing in early childhood development. Proven record in establishing and delivering systems providing quality day care.

EXPERIENCE

BURLINGTON FAMILY DAYCARE, Burlington, Vermont

Field Supervisor, 1988 - present

Supervise a case load of 40 day care providers for satellite family day care system. Screen potential providers through one-on-one interview, telephone interview with provider's husband, and a home evaluation. Orient potential parents to program through office interview. Place children in provider homes.

Conduct monthly visits to providers. Offer technical assistance and plan professional development and growth. Monitor children's progress.

Establish effective communication with parents; address special needs for children and offer encouragement and support. Write bi-annual progress reports for each child and conduct telephone conferences with parents.

Check and update provider and child files and document new providers. Assist in administering USDA food program.

Participate in provider meetings, workshops, and parent workshops.

TEACHING EXPERIENCE

BURLINGTON PUBLIC SCHOOLS, Burlington, Vermont
  Third Grade Teacher, Middle Ridge Elementary School, 1983 - 1988
  Fifth Grade Teacher, Lemon Tree Elementary School, 1980 - 1983

BOSTON PUBLIC SCHOOLS, Boston, Massachusetts
  Fourth Grade Teacher, Green Hills Elementary School, 1978 - 1980

EDUCATION

M.ED., Boston University, Boston, Massachusetts, 1980

B.A., Education, Castleton State College, Castleton, Vermont, 1976

PAULINE PARKER

97 Elm Street
Bloomington, Indiana 47401
Work (812) 999-XXXX Home (812) 888-XXXX

SUMMARY OF QUALIFICATIONS

Registered Dietitian with broad experience with corporate, community, and public sector organizations.

- Energetic, enthusiastic, results-oriented professional who loves working with people.

- Extensive experience developing and delivering a wide range of nutrition programs while making learning fun.

EXPERIENCE

CHIEF CLINICAL DIETITIAN, 1988 - present
Willow Hospital, Bloomington, Indiana

Plan and administer patient care and education, in-service and interdepartmental training, menu planning, and outpatient clinic. Interview, select, and supervise two registered dietitians and four diet clerks; train staff and evaluate performance.

- Developed policies and procedures and new therapeutic diets; reviewed and revised diet manual and policy and procedures manual. Assisted in preparing *Total Prenatal Nutrition* manual.

- Taught a series of diabetic classes offered by the diabetic teaching team and a series of weight management classes.

- Developed and taught seminar on the myths and facts of nutrition for the athlete.

- Researched and implemented Healthy Hearts Kitchen classes. Participated in prenatal classes, offered to young, low-income groups.

NUTRITION WELLNESS EDUCATOR, 1985 - 1987

Conducted a variety of nutrition wellness programs for corporations and other organizations in the Indianapolis metropolitan area.

- Contributed expertise to American Heart Association programs and other community organizations. Led workshops, participated at health fairs, demonstrated healthy cooking, and acted as radio/television spokesperson.

FOOD SERVICE DIRECTOR, 1982 - 1985
Village Nursing Home, Greenfield, Indiana

Performed management responsibilities for both clinical and administrative activities for a staff of 20. Planned, directed, and administered patient care and education and outpatient counseling. Supervised staff of 12 - 15 employees; hired, trained, evaluated performance. Conducted in-service training.

- Scheduled staff, planned menus. Supervised food ordering and production. Reviewed and revised diet manual and policy and procedure manual.

CHIEF CLINICAL DIETITIAN, 1978 - 1981
Greenfield Hospital Center, Greenfield, Indiana

Supervised two dietitians and four diet clerks. Coordinated patient care and education, outpatient clinic, weight control classes, and inter- and intra-departmental training.

- Assisted in developing and revising policies and procedures, therapeutic diets, and menu planning.

EDUCATION

B.S., Dietetics, Purdue University, West Lafayette, Indiana

Dietetic Internship, Purdue University Medical Center, West Lafayette, Indiana

PROFESSIONAL DEVELOPMENT

Certified Leader

"Choose to Lose" weight management program
Regional Training Workshops, "Healthy Hearts Kitchen Course"
"Lifesteps" weight management program

CERTIFICATION

Registered Dietitian
Licensed Dietitian, Indiana

PROFESSIONAL ASSOCIATIONS

American Dietetic Association
Indiana Dietetic Association
Consulting Nutritionists in the Indianapolis Area

CAROLINE BELL
5 Paradise Lane, Houston, Texas 77060
Work (713) 544-XXXX Home (713) 533-XXXX

CAREER SUMMARY

Extensive experience in display and merchandising in a variety of work environments. Apply innovative ideas and solutions and a creative approach to each assignment.

EXPERIENCE

DISPLAY MANAGER, 1992 - present
   Simpsons Department Store, Houston, Texas

Create visual excitement throughout the store and contribute to sales goal achievement by designing innovative window and department displays. Review new merchandise and develop unique store themes, special events, and corporate promotions. Manage staff of six.

DEPARTMENT MANAGER, 1988 - 1992
   Brown's, Houston, Texas

Managed gourmet section for home furnishings specialty store. Created attractive displays and successfully coordinated promotional themes resulting in increased department sales. Managed staff of four.

STORE MANAGER, 1985 - 1988
   Artistic Frames and Gallery, Dallas, Texas

Supervised selecting, framing, and displaying retail prints and antique botanicals. Cut, built, and assembled frames. Developed clientele and increased sales.

MANAGER, 1984 - 1985
   Scenic Art Gallery, Phoenix, Arizona

Managed gallery shop, produced effective and attractive displays, and coordinated ten major openings. Assisted in layout and typesetting of monthly newsletter and designed advertisements for local papers. Generated new ideas for special "Scenic Art Gallery" products such as T-shirts, posters, and calendars.

EDUCATION

Fine Arts and Graphic studies at University of Arizona and Parsons School of Design

CATHERINE T. ARNOLD

7 Pleasant Street
Atlanta, Georgia 30309
Work (404) 777-XXXX Home (404) 555-XXXX

CAREER SUMMARY

Broad background in all aspects of the publishing process with specific knowledge and experience in editing and graphic design.

Managerial expertise, extensive desktop publishing experience, excellent organization and communication skills.

EXPERIENCE

EXECUTIVE EDITOR   1988 - present

Plan and direct production of *Medical Voice*, the international journal of the Association of Medical Administrators, with circulation of 50,000 readers in over 100 countries.

Manage staff of six. Oversee editorial and strategic planning, editing and advertising, circulation and graphic design. Establish effective working relationships with authors and an international committee.

MANAGING EDITOR   1984 - 1988

Progressed from freelance editor to full-time staff at Southern Publications. Edited an entertainment memorabilia publication, *Flash*. Increased circulation by more than 500% and quadrupled page count during tenure.

FREELANCE EDITOR AND WRITER   1980 - 1984

Edited textbooks and educational materials, a national pharmacy journal, various newsletters, research reports, and art books.

Wrote more than 1,000 articles for magazines and newspapers. Wrote a weekly column for a daily newspaper, the *Atlanta Voice*.

RESEARCHER   1979 - 1980

Awarded research grant from National Endowment for the Humanities. Conducted research on the scope and significance of corporate art collections in America.

ADMINISTRATOR   1977 - 1979

Coordinated a learning laboratory and several learning programs at Southern Community College, designed to supplement and enhance classroom instruction.

TEACHER   1965 - 1977

Held numerous teaching positions at the college and high school level; art consultant to an elementary school.

EDUCATION

Ph.D., Curriculum and Instruction, EMORY UNIVERSITY, Atlanta, Georgia

M.A., Humanities, TULANE UNIVERSITY, New Orleans, Louisiana

B.A., Art and English, DUKE UNIVERSITY, Durham, North Carolina

ROBERTA ST. JOHN
Certified Internal Auditor

855 Country Club Court
Palo Alto, California 94304

Work (415) 444-XXXX
Home (415) 333-XXXX

EXPERIENCE

ABC CORPORATION, Palo Alto, California
Senior EDP Auditor, 1987 - present

Ensure the integrity of system software in an Amdahl 5990, DEC 6210, and Tandem environment. Perform reviews of system software; evaluate adequacy of installation options, processing controls, and audit trails. Systems include MVS, CICS, Telecommunications, Top Secret Security, and TMS.

♦ Conduct application reviews of systems developed by data processing to evaluate system integrity, audit trails, controls, and documentation including profit and loss and points-of-sale (POS).

♦ Provide computer programming support for operational auditors, external auditors, and senior management. Major projects include recalculation of employee stock distribution, inventory exposure reports, inventory price test, and analysis of customers' purchases and payments.

♦ Train internal auditors in the use of Easytrieve Plus, Panaudit Plus, TSO/ISPF, and SDSF and EDP auditors in auditing and workpaper techniques.

♦ Ensure the long-range EDP audit schedule is accurate and up-to-date.

♦ Perform operational audits of out-of-town warehouses and distribution centers and test for compliance with corporate policies and procedures. Identify cost saving areas.

CALIFORNIA BANK GROUP, San Francisco, California
EDP Auditor, 1986 - 1987

Assistant to EDP Audit Manager of small audit department working within an IBM DOS environment.

♦ Developed comprehensive audit programs for performing application, data center, and minicomputer reviews, and computer audit programs to help support financial auditors using **Easytrieve Plus.**

♦ Performed EDP general controls and application reviews to evaluate controls.

CALIFORNIA BANKSHARES, San Francisco, California
EDP Auditor/System Analyst, 1984 - 1986

Member of Audit Support Staff of a multi-million dollar bank holding company working within an IBM DOS/VSE and OS/MVS environment.

♦ Performed reviews of systems under development and application conversion projects to determine adequacy of system controls and audit trails. Recommended modifications to ensure compliance with government regulations.

♦ Supervised audit staff of programmers, coordinated staff assignments and training, and ensured work conformed to departmental standards.

GOLDEN GATE BANK, San Francisco, California
EDP Auditor, 1983 - 1984

Served on small team charged with assuring the security and data integrity of all EDP systems working within a Burroughs 4800 environment.

♦ Developed and maintained programs to support the audit functions including branch audits, loan reviews, year-end reviews, and operational audits.

♦ Created a comprehensive manual detailing all steps involved in utilizing the on-line computer system and audit software.

Programmer/Analyst, 1981 - 1983

Designed computer programs to meet specific needs of bank's trust department.

♦ Automated the function of preparing customer's end of fiscal year statements of condition and trial balance; developed file specifications, data entry procedures, report layouts, and user manuals. Trained users in system use.

TECHNICAL SKILLS

Hardware

AMDAHL, IBM MVS/XA, DEC, VAX, TANDEM, PC

Software

SAS, Easytrieve Plus, COBOL, TSO/ISPF, Roscoe, CICS, Top Secret, SDSF, JES2, IBM JCL, IBM Utilities, Librarian

EDUCATION

Bachelor of Science, major Statistics, minor Computer Science, 1981
San Francisco State University, San Francisco, California

CERTIFICATIONS

Certified Internal Auditor
Certified Data Processor

MICHAEL P. SCOTT
9 Shady Street, Silver Spring, Maryland 20905
(301) 921-XXXX

CAREER HISTORY

Over 40 years of experience in the design, training, field engineering, and plant start-up and operational phases of both BWR and PWR nuclear power plants.

- Developed an expertise and advised suppliers, users, and NRC on the design, construction, and operational phases of various nuclear power plants.

- Managed major nuclear projects and provided resolution to a wide range of plant and reactor systems problems.

EXPERIENCE

U. S. Nuclear Regulatory Commission (NRC), Bethesda, Maryland
SENIOR ELECTRICAL ENGINEER, 1969 - 1990

Total responsibility for implementation of the plant modifications required by "ATWS-rule." Reviewed the plant specific submittals on the design for the "Diverse Scram System" (DSS) and the "ATWS Mitigating Actuating Circuitry" (AMSAC). Made presentations on controversial issues to NRC management, ACRS, and CRGR including the independent power source issue involving B&W type power plants and the equipment diversity issue involving the BWR type power plants. Both were resolved at the Executive Office level.

Performed evaluations and inspections of highly complex technical issues and problems. Ensured conformance to the applicable regulations and guidelines as outlined in Chapter 7 of the Standard Review Plan (SRP) and prepared safety evaluation and inspection reports. Issued safety evaluation and technical position reports.

Accomplishments

- NRC Special Achievement Awards, 1985, 1988, and 1990.

- Selected as the evaluator and technical advisor and monitor during development of the electrical/instrumentation training courses offered by the NRC Training Center in Chattanooga, Tennessee.

- Selected as an augmented inspection team (AIT) member formed to review and evaluate the licensees' actions regarding the "Failed Reactor Trip Breaker" event at D.C. Cook Power Plant. As a result, IEB-85-02 was issued requiring corrective actions by the affected power plants.

- Author and Task Manager of activities surrounding IE Bulletin 79-01B, *Environmental Qualification of Electrical Equipment*. The work group issued a total of 53 technical evaluation reports (TERs) forming acceptance guidelines for on-going environmental qualification issues.

- Selected as team leader of the task group formed to develop a TI to inspect licensees' actions for meeting the guidelines specified in Regulatory Guide 1.97-Post Accident Monitoring Instrumentation.

- Conducted site visits to the Hope Creek and Salem Nuclear Power Plants. Issued NRC-Bulletin 90-01.

- Evaluated and issued report on the licensee's procedures for calibrating non-adjustable process measurement sensors (RTD's and TCs) at Cooper Nuclear Station.

General Public Utilities, Nuclear Power Activities Group, Parsippany, New Jersey
CONSULTANT SPECIALIST-INSTRUMENTATION & CONTROL, 1968 - 1969

Monitored all nuclear power activities related to electrical, instrumentation, and controls for reactor plants under construction such as Three Mile Island Units 1 and 2, Oyster Creek Unit 1, and the proposed Forked River Unit 1. Assisted with the pre-operational and start-up testing programs for electrical and instrumentation at the Oyster Creek Reactor Site.

Allis Chalmers, Atomic Power Division, Washington, D. C.
SENIOR NUCLEAR ENGINEER-INSTRUMENTATION AND CONTROL, 1958 - 1968

Lead Electrical and Instrumentation & Controls (I&C) Engineer for the LaCrosse Boiling Water Reactor (LABWR). Lead responsibility for the design, field construction, and testing of the process, electrical distribution, and control systems for the Elk River Reactor. Performed pre-operational system tests and instructed utility personnel for AEC-Licensed Reactor Operators exam.

AMF Atomics, Atomic Power Department, Greenwich, Connecticut
INSTRUMENTATION AND CONTROLS ENGINEER, 1957 - 1958

Assisted in the conceptual design and development of nuclear, radiation, and process instrumentation systems and the in-plant electrical power distribution system for a closed cycle boiling water reactor.

Westinghouse Electric, Atomic Power Division (Bettis) Navy Program, Bettis, Pennsylvania
TEST AND OPERATING ENGINEER, 1949 - 1957

Performed test and operating engineering functions; verified the reliability of major components such as pumps, valves, electrical components, and specialized instrumentation for the USS Nautilus prototype reactor plant.

PROFESSIONAL DEVELOPMENT

"Electrical Equipment Testing and Maintenance," George Washington University
Instrument Training Schools, Bailey, Foxboro, General Electric, and Westinghouse
"Nuclear Power Safety," MIT
"PWR Systems," Westinghouse
"BWR Systems," USNRC
"Reliability and Fault Tree Analysis," USNRC
"Human Factors Engineering," USNRC
"Reliability In Nuclear Power Generating Stations," IEEE
"Effective Briefing Techniques," USDA
"Reviewing and Editing," USNRC

EDUCATION

B.S. Engineering-Electronics, Clarkson University, Potsdam, New York

TECHNICAL SOCIETIES

Participated in the IEEE Work Group Committee that developed the approved Standard, IEEE 336-1971. Former member of the American Nuclear Society and the Instrument Society of America.

CLEARANCES

"Q," "Air Force Top Secret," and "L" clearances

NICHOLAS R. FIELD
76 Sandstone Court, Livermore, California 94551 (510) 666-XXXX

ELECTRICAL ENGINEER SPECIALIZING IN ELECTRICAL BUILDING DESIGN, POWER, AND COMMUNICATION SYSTEMS.

EDUCATION

Bachelor of Science, Electrical Engineering, 1993
COLORADO TECHNICAL COLLEGE, Colorado Springs, Colorado
Communications Courses:
Fiber Optics & Applications, Satellite Communications, Radio Engineering I & II
Power Courses:
Power System Theory Design, Power System Protection
Certified Engineer-in-Training, states of Colorado and California

COMPUTER SKILLS

Programming in FORTRAN, Pascal, BASIC
Knowledge of WordPerfect, Lotus 1-2-3, PSPICE, AutoCAD

RELATED EXPERIENCE

HENRY HILL & ASSOCIATES, Livermore, California
Building Electrical Engineer, 1993

Effectively contributed to team engineering projects. Designed, evaluated, and drafted electrical distribution of power for numerous office building tenants.

Successfully produced preliminary roadway lighting design for the Highway 15 Extension Project.

Developed preliminary parking area lighting design for the Livermore Convention Center Project.

CITY OF DENVER, Denver, Colorado
Engineering Intern, 1992

Completed four-month internship, assisting in a variety of engineering projects.

CHANNEL 70-LIVERMORE COMMUNITY TELEVISION, Livermore, California
Volunteer Engineer, Summers 1991 - 1992

Assisted staff engineer on various communication projects.

SUMMER EXPERIENCE

LIVERMORE OFFICE SUPPLY CORPORATION, Livermore, California
Office Assistant, Summers 1988 - 1992

Developed and utilized skills in effective customer relations. Assisted customers in identifying and satisfying their office product needs.

PROFESSIONAL AFFILIATIONS

National Society of Professional Engineers
Institute of Electrical and Electronics Engineers

JOHN K. IRWIN
7 Rolling Lane, Potomac, Maryland 20854
Office (202) 777-XXXX Home (301) 999-XXXX

CAREER HISTORY

Expert in environmental procedures and policies with an expertise in interpreting and communicating information clearly, concisely, and professionally to 10 regional offices and 40 field offices of Department of Housing and Urban Development (HUD).

Focal point in providing guidance and assistance to local communities, enabling their compliance with environmental review and procedural requirements of the National Environmental Policy Act (NEPA) with respect to the Community Development Block Grant Program, the HOME, HOPE and Homeless programs, and the CHAS requirements of Affordable Housing.

EXPERIENCE

DEPARTMENT OF HOUSING AND URBAN DEVELOPMENT, Washington, D.C.

ENVIRONMENTAL PLANNING OFFICER, 1979 - present

- Interpret environmental policies and procedures and provide guidance to federal, state, and local communities to ensure compliance with environmental regulations.

- Provide technical assistance to communities concerning site-specific and the NEPA related Federal statutes such as Historic Preservation, Flood Plain Management, Flood Insurance requirements, and the toxic-waste and storage-sensitive areas.

- Develop policy guides and advisory materials to assist field offices in their performance.

- Revise HUD's environmental regulations (24 CFR Part 58), resulting in more effective and comprehensive guidance rather than on the present program-by-program basis.

- Review HUD issuances, competitive grant applications, and complete special assignments related to field office problems requiring unique and specialized solutions.

- Monitor and evaluate field office performance.

RELATED EXPERIENCE

Directed a technical assistance project for National Savings & Loan League, East African Office, designed to assist East African and Southwest Asian countries in the development of their National Housing Policies, 1975 - 1978.

Taught graduate courses in the Division of Environmental and Urban Systems at Virginia Polytechnic Institute & State University, 1973 - 1975.

EDUCATION

Ph.D. in Metropolitan Studies, Harvard University-School of Design, Cambridge, Massachusetts
M.S. in Urban Planning, Boston University, Boston, Massachusetts
B.S. in Landscape Architecture, Cornell University, Ithaca, New York

SENIOR ACCOUNTANT, 1989 - 1992

Managed the daily general ledger operations to ensure accurate and timely financial information. Performed and supervised all accounting functions, coordinating and confirming that Accounts Receivable, Accounts Payable, Inventory, and Payroll systems transactions were properly reflected. Organized interim and year-end audits. Provided external auditors with all required financial documentation. Trained and supervised one professional.

- Enhanced general ledger, report writer, cost allocation, and ratio analysis modules of LAWSON software. Streamlined routine functions and improved usefulness of standardized software by developing enhancements.

- Increased the timeliness of the general ledger close by 66%. Headed conversion of new general ledger system.

- Restructured company's general ledger into a comprehensive framework, enabling it to meet medium- and long-term needs.

- Identified weaknesses in internal control for reimbursement from parent company for aircraft demonstrator tour program. Initiated, developed, and implemented a policy ensuring all future recoveries.

Health Plus Inc., Costa Mesa, California, 1987 - 1989

SENIOR ACCOUNTANT, 1988 - 1989

Promoted from Staff Accountant. Coordinated all aspects of SEC reporting for multi-million dollar health maintenance organization. Prepared all debt covenant reporting to financial institutions and internal financial reports to management. Trained and supervised one professional.

- Implemented FAS 95 Statement of Cash Flows as required by the SEC.

STAFF ACCOUNTANT, 1987 - 1988

Reviewed and analyzed financial statements of 6 major subsidiaries comprising 25% of total revenue. Assisted with all facets of SEC reporting, including consolidated financial statements, supporting schedules, and footnotes. Maintained nationwide company's chart of accounts. Resolved all general ledger coding issues.

- Developed automated system to monitor reconciliation responsibilities of 2,000 general ledger accounts. Designed and presented seminar to educate employees on general ledger coding procedures.

EDUCATION

Candidate for Master in Business Administration, degree expected September 1994
San Diego State University, San Diego, California

Bachelor of Science in Accounting, 1986
University of California, Irvine, Irvine, California
One of five recipients of the **Outstanding Student Award**, College of Business

CERTIFICATION

Certified Public Accountant

LEWIS EDWARDS
75 Rambling Lane
Lansing, Michigan 48909
(517) 333-XXXX

BACKGROUND SUMMARY

A dedicated and professional fire service officer. Effective manager, motivating personnel and increasing productivity while elevating morale. Expertise in coordinating and directing fire/life safety and prevention programs.

FIRE AND EMERGENCY SERVICE EXPERIENCE

Assistant Fire Chief
   LANSING FIRE DISTRICT, Lansing, Michigan, 1990 - present

Direct operations and personnel for fire suppression and emergency medical rescue. Manage fire marshall, 2 officers, and 27 fire personnel; conduct staff training and continuing education.

Supervise supply, maintenance, and suppression functions for 9-piece combination department. Assist with fiscal management, fire prevention, and arson investigations.

- Developed training programs and minimum training standards for volunteer fire fighters.

- Established a full-time Fire Prevention/Fire Safety Education Bureau.

- Implemented a management team concept that developed the department from its beginning stages into an effective, efficient organization.

Division Chief
   GRAND RAPIDS FIRE DISTRICT, Grand Rapids, Michigan, 1985 - 1990

Created, instituted, operated, and managed a 911 Emergency Communications Center that answered and processed 200,000 law enforcement, fire, and EMS incidents.

Supervised a staff of 30 captains and dispatchers in a division with an annual budget of $800,000. Prepared budget and monitored expenditures.

- Developed and implemented a county-wide Computer Aided Dispatch system and a Standard Operating Procedure Manual.

- Set up a 900-hour Certified Fire-Medic Dispatcher Training Program. Designed and conducted a staff stress management program.

Lieutenant
   KALAMAZOO VALLEY FIRE DEPARTMENT, Kalamazoo, Michigan, 1981 - 1985

Held progressive positions from public relations officer, training instructor, driver-engineer to fire fighter. Supervised a 3-piece, 40-member company and served as first line company suppression officer.

- Created a "First Recruit" training program, including manuals and slide presentation. Wrote monthly training bulletins.

VOLUNTEER FIRE SERVICE EXPERIENCE

MICHIGAN FIRE MUTUAL AID ASSOCIATION, Lansing, Michigan
President, 1992 - present
Secretary/Treasurer, 1991
Chairman, Professional Development, 1990

FLINT FIRE CONTROL DISTRICT, Flint, Michigan
Lieutenant, 1980 - 1981
Fire Fighter, 1978 - 1980

EDUCATION

Associate in Science, Fire Service, 1981
LANSING COMMUNITY COLLEGE, Lansing, Michigan

Fire Service Continued Education
Courses in **Arson and Incendiary Devices, Blitz Attack, Rural Fire Fighting and Tanker Operations, Fire Behavior and Building Construction**, and **Incident Command.**

AWARDS

Meritorious Service Award, Lansing Fire District, 1992
Achievement Award, Grand Rapids Fire District, 1990
Extraordinary Service Award, Grand Rapids Fire District, 1988

ASSOCIATIONS

International Association of Fire Chiefs
National Fire Protection Association
Michigan Fire Chiefs' Association

MAURICE PIERRE MOLLE
5 Bishop Lane
Appleton, Wisconsin 54910
(414) 444-XXXX

CAREER SUMMARY

Extensive foreign service experience in third world countries. Expertise in managing multi-disciplinary and multi-national staffs and contractors.

- Excellent communication, interpersonal, speaking, and writing skills.

- Successful in planning, organizing, and completing projects utilizing effective problem-solving techniques.

- Knowledge of resources and organizations active in foreign assistance.

RELATED EXPERIENCE

U.S. AGENCY FOR INTERNATIONAL DEVELOPMENT (A.I.D.), 1966 - 1992

CHIEF OF PROGRAM OPERATIONS, Senegal, 1984 - 1992

Supervised country-specific assistance planning program averaging $50 million annually. Designed and implemented innovative models and procedures for bi-lateral agreements. Managed U.S. economist, five Senegalese professionals, and four support staff (one French, one Syrian, two Senegalese.)

Achieved an unbroken, four-year pattern of trouble-free international funding and assistance agreements in both English and French.

Produced and submitted major annual reports from field missions for Washington and Congressional approvals. Conducted, reviewed, and approved project evaluations. Prepared and obtained U.S. and host country approvals for all A.I.D.-financed development assistance.

Edited, revised, and approved requests from mission elements for all A.I.D.-financed technical assistance contracts under A.I.D.-financed assistance programs, and backstopped all mission monitoring of such contracts. Led implementation of a computerized planning, monitoring, and reporting system.

PROGRAM OFFICER, Mauritania, 1982 - 1984

Supervised country-specific assistance planning program averaging $10 million annually. Managed two U.S. professionals, two personal services contract experts (one Canadian, one French), and four support staff (one American, Mauritian, Filipino, and Mauritanian.)

Successfully managed agriculture program despite severe constraints imposed by agriculture ministry. Coordinated re-design and approval of roads project.

STUDENT, Rosslyn, Virginia, 1981 - 1982

Attended U.S. Foreign Service Institute in French language program.

ASSISTANT AGRICULTURAL DEVELOPMENT OFFICER, Yemen Arab Republic, 1980 - 1981
ASSISTANT PROGRAM OFFICER, Yemen Arab Republic, 1979 - 1980

Conducted major evaluation of U.S.-financed assistance to establishing and staffing an agriculture secondary school. Re-designed important project coordinated with agriculture ministry. Co-supervised two U.S. professionals and one Yemeni professional.

ASSISTANT PROGRAM OFFICER, Washington, D.C., 1977 - 1979

Processed documentation for all centrally funded U.S. support for the 15 International Agricultural Research Centers.

STUDENT, Rosslyn, Virginia, 1977

Attended U.S. Foreign Service Institute Economic and Commercial Studies Program.

ASSISTANT PROGRAM OFFICER, El Salvador, 1975 - 1977

STUDENT, Rosslyn, Virginia, 1975

Attended U.S. Foreign Service Institute Spanish language program.

ASSISTANT PROGRAM OFFICER, Bangkok, Thailand, 1970 - 1974
FIELD EVALUATION OFFICER, Saigon, South Vietnam, 1968 - 1969
REFUGEE AFFAIRS OFFICER, South Vietnam, 1966 - 1968

CIVIC EXPERIENCE

Involved from 1988 to present in various civic projects including: Literacy Action Council, High School District Planning, U.S. Census, Amateur Theater, and Community Public Speaking.

EDUCATION

Bachelor of Arts, major in Government, University of Wisconsin, Madison, Wisconsin

SKILLS

Moderate fluency in French, Spanish, Vietnamese, and German
Proficient with IBM PC and WordPerfect

ROBERT W. BOLTON

77 Glade Way, Rockville, Maryland 20852   (301)555-XXXX

QUALIFICATIONS SUMMARY: Anticipate problems and devise solutions for diverse assignments throughout the world. Highly effective research techniques and oral and written communication skills.

EXPERIENCE

Foreign Service Specialist/Agent

U.S. Department of State, Washington, D.C., 1981 - present

> Progressive assignments and expertise in the foreign service and intelligence community. Conduct wide range of research and investigations. Plan, organize, and execute complicated assignments. Formulate strategic management policy and procedures. Solve problems by identifying fraud, waste, and mismanagement.

> Developed and implemented international and domestic security plans for the Secretary of State and foreign dignitaries. Created communication links for around-the-clock coverage. Established effective relationships within the security and protective service community. Collected and utilized intelligence information.

> Assumed overall responsibility and successfully handled crisis situation in a dangerous posting, U.S. Embassy Beirut. Designed a physical security plan and supervised implementation in a chaotic work environment. Managed large diverse staff including civilians, U.S. Military, and foreign nationals. Received **Meritorious Valor Award** and **Superior Honor Award.**

> Conducted background investigations for presidential appointments and foreign service personnel.

Supervisor of Investigations

Montgomery County Police Department, Bethesda, Maryland, 1974 - 1980

> Supervised staff of investigators and office personnel. Coordinated investigations of allegations of excessive force by members of Montgomery County Police Department; personally handled the most sensitive cases.

State Attorney's Investigator

Baltimore Attorney's Office, Baltimore, Maryland, 1971 - 1974

> Assisted Prosecutor in conducting research and investigations for organized crime and financial crime units.

Military Police Investigator

U.S. Army, Republic of South Vietnam, 1969 - 1970

> Conducted investigation of felonies. Received **Army Commendation Medal**.

EDUCATION

Bachelor of Science in Education, University of Maryland, College Park, Maryland, 1968

AMELIA BOND

22 Amarillo Boulevard, Houston, Texas 77058
(713) 666-XXXX

SUMMARY OF QUALIFICATIONS

Extensive experience in Fund Raising and Meeting and Event Planning activities. Imaginative and creative with the ability to communicate and deal effectively with individuals at all organizational levels.

RELATED EXPERIENCE

FUND RAISING

Participate on committees of at least five annual charity events. Involved in planning, organizing, soliciting, and coordinating arrangements.

- Conceptualized with Saks Firth Avenue, the "Great Catalogue Caper," a fund raiser now featured as a major benefit in eight different areas of the United States.
- Member of the National Fund Raising Committee of the American Cancer Society.
- Member of the Board of the American Cancer Society, Houston affiliate, as Chairman of the Committee for Fund Raising.
- Division Chairman for Southside Hospital Building Campaign. Supervised 5 captains and 50 workers in fund raising motivation and implementation to meet division goal of $3.8 million.
- Co-chaired Texan Hospital Relief Tenth Anniversary Gala.

PROGRAM PLANNING

Served on boards of various organizations including: Mental Health Association, General Federation of Women's Clubs, and Boy Scouts of America.

- International luncheon series, Houston Club
  Secured dignitaries to speak at ten monthly luncheons.
- The Hospitality and Information Services, Diplomacy International
  As Committee Chairman and Officer, planned and chaired events and tours for member of the Diplomatic community.
- Heritage Day, Houston Symphony
  Recruited and scheduled 78 women to hostess at the Symphony Ball.
- Houston Music Club
  Promoted the Music Club for six years and chaired the "Salute to Arts" Benefit Committee. Served on the Board as Chairman of Patrons and Sponsors and scheduled the fund raising solicitation process.
- Cultural Day, Houston Woman's Club
  Member of the Organizing Committee. Recruited and entertained Committee.
- Muriel Samuels Home, Houston, Texas
  Program Chairman of Junior Board; planned and executed all programs for 175 residents including films, teas, and lectures.
- Beachwood Woman's Club
  As 2nd Vice President for 700 member organization, chaired Program Committee and planned over 40 programs per year.

MEMBERSHIPS

The Houston Club
Women's Economic Alliance Foundation
Daughters of the American Revolution
The Hospitality and Information Service

Houston Speakers Club
National Society of Arts and Letters
Houston Ballet Woman's Committee

HARRIET HARRINGTON

99 Park Terrace, Wilmington, Delaware 19898
(302) 445-XXXX

QUALIFICATION SUMMARY

Broad range of experience in the health care business environment. Highly successful in developing and establishing new business within the health care community.

Recognized specialist in occupational health as a clinician, manager, and administrator.

EXPERIENCE

ADMINISTRATOR
Quick Medical Care of Wilmington, Inc., Wilmington, Delaware

Established an ambulatory care center operating 98 hours/week. Direct responsibility for contract negotiations, business/personnel management, and clinical coordination. Recruited, hired, and trained initial staff of 30.

Created administrative and accounting systems/procedures as well as those involving clinical activities, laboratory, and X-ray. Supervised Accounts Payable and Accounts Receivable with other financial responsibilities including budgeting, cash flow, and bank transactions.

Developed and implemented annual marketing plan and coordinated effective media/communications campaign. Conducted seminar presentations and handled public relations activities. Overall responsibility for equipment purchase, maintenance contracts, and facility management.

EXECUTIVE DIRECTOR
Women's Health Network, Inc., Mercy Hospital, Newark, Delaware

Developed and directed a hospital-based, self-referral, mobile mammography screening program. Generated and implemented marketing plan, negotiated contracts, and prepared proposals. Managed corporate sales, coordinated effective media/communications campaign, conducted educational seminars, and handled public relations activities.

OCCUPATIONAL HEALTH/NURSE PRACTITIONER ADMINISTRATOR
Johns Hopkins University School of Medicine, Baltimore, Maryland

Provided on-site occupational health services for employees. Assessed needs, planned, implemented, and evaluated the program. Created a stress management program and designed and implemented a wellness/health promotion program for the staff. Taught undergraduate level in nursing and second-year medical students. Acted as nurse practitioner and clinical preceptor for eliciting and recording patient history.

EDUCATION

UNIVERSITY OF DELAWARE SCHOOL OF NURSING, Newark, Delaware
Bachelor of Science in Nursing
Primary Care Adult Nurse Practitioner Program, Certificate

LICENSES AND CERTIFICATES

R.N. - Delaware, Maryland
N.P. - Delaware, Maryland
American Nurses' Association - Certified Adult Nurse Practitioner (RN-C)
American Board of Occupational Health Nurses, Certified Occupational Health Nurse (COHN)

FRANCINE H. GRANT
88 Belleview Street, Kansas City, Missouri 64108
(816) 222-XXXX

QUALIFICATIONS SUMMARY

Wide range of experience as health care educator and practitioner. Excellent interpersonal and written communication skills. Adept in selecting appropriate resources and delivering education programs to meet diverse needs.

PROFESSIONAL EXPERIENCE AND ACCOMPLISHMENTS

HEALTH EDUCATION

- Educated elementary and high school students; taught health classes on wide range of medical topics including AIDS Awareness, First-Aid, Cardiac Wellness, Safety, and Nutrition.
- Taught two-hour Red Cross-certified course in HIV/AIDS Awareness.
- Initiated "Sports Team Trainer Program" for mature high school students. Trained and certified them in CPR, First-Aid, and instructed in relevant topics on sports injury.
- Developed and co-moderated discussion group for 7th graders on teenage issues.
- Organized and implemented an alcohol and drug abuse prevention retreat program for teenagers.
- Implemented district program establishing Fitness Club for overweight elementary school students.

CLINICAL NURSING

- Performed nursing responsibilities in busy multi-practice pediatric office. Administered immunizations, allergy treatment medications, prepped and read lab samples. Assisted physicians in emergency and routine care. Conducted parenting education.
- As Head Nurse, administered nursing care in 20-bed pediatric unit. Identified daily staffing needs and scheduled staff to meet patient requirements. Wrote and conducted staff evaluations. Handled admitting process and provided quality nursing care.
- Furnished emergency medical care as part of community rescue team.

COMMUNITY NURSING

- Provided health care, with power of attorney responsibility for medical and dental, for 300 boarding students, ages 12-18, from around the world.
- Oversaw preventative and emergency care of elementary students and staff in schools ranging from 300-800 students. Conducted health screening and identified at-risk students in community as member of Child Study Committee. Participated in Family Advocacy Committee, a multi-disciplinary committee sponsored by military commands. Supervised and trained 2 health aides.

WORK HISTORY

CERTIFIED RED CROSS INSTRUCTOR
Westlake High School, Kansas City, Missouri, 1991
Marlow Field School, St. Louis, Missouri, 1988 - 1991

SCHOOL NURSE
Marlow Field School, St. Louis, Missouri, 1988 - 1991
Marlow Elementary School, St. Louis, Missouri, 1987 - 1988
St. Louis School System, St. Louis, Missouri, 1983 - 1986

OFFICE NURSE
Pediatrics Association, St. Louis, Missouri, 1983 - 1986

RESCUE SQUAD MEMBER
St. Louis Fire & Rescue, St. Louis, Missouri, 1974 - 1975

HEAD NURSE
General Hospital, Independence, Missouri, 1968 - 1969

EDUCATION

GENERAL HOSPITAL SCHOOL OF NURSING, Independence, Missouri
Diploma, Registered Nurse, 1967

PROFESSIONAL DEVELOPMENT

Crisis Intervention in Child Abuse and Rape, University of Missouri, Kansas City, Missouri

School Nursing Principles & Practice, St. Louis University, St. Louis, Missouri

Emergency Care Nursing, St. Louis University, St. Louis, Missouri

Audiology Workshop, St. Louis Hearing & Speech Center, St. Louis, Missouri

Scoliosis Update, St. Louis University, St. Louis, Missouri

LICENSES

Registered Nurse, Missouri

CERTIFICATION

American Red Cross Certification
Standard First-Aid/CPR, HIV/AIDS Education, Basic AIDS Training

KATHERINE CAMPBELL
9 Briar Way, Phoenix, Arizona 85003
(602) 888-XXXX

HUMAN RESOURCES/EMPLOYEE RELATIONS MANAGEMENT

A results-oriented human resources manager with progressively increasing responsibility. Extensive experience in building relationships, articulating visions, and implementing goals and objectives.

CAREER HIGHLIGHTS

- Directed human resources functions for 17 high technology groups throughout U.S., Asia, and Europe.

- Negotiated labor agreements with 15 international presidents of the AFL-CIO, resulting in cost savings in excess of $8 million.

- Won 97% of arbitration cases.

- Reduced health and welfare benefit program costs annually by $100,000 while maintaining level of benefits.

- Reformulated pension and 401(k) plans, yielding $426,000 annually.

- Successfully sustained company's position in an Office Federal Contract Compliance review targeting executive compensation and prerequisites.

- Implemented HAY Compensation pay program for 10,000 employees.

SUMMARY OF SKILLS AND EXPERTISE

- Directed the recruitment, interview, and selection process for high technology companies.

- Created and instituted training and development programs, employee relations programs, and performance management and assessment programs.

- Facilitated organizational design, development, and implementation programs.

- Introduced flexible benefit programs; developed and executed EEO/AAP plans for reviews without deficiencies.

- Established job evaluation and compensation programs; reduced turn-over rates and increased retention.

- Developed effective procedure manuals and employee handbooks.

- Established creative relocation and incentive programs.

- Administered OSHA, NRC Safety Reporting and Compliance programs.

WORK HISTORY

Human Resources Manager, ADD International, Phoenix, Arizona, 1990 - 1993
Technical Personnel Director, Software Ltd., Tucson, Arizona, 1988 - 1990
Employee Relations Manager, Phoenix Utilities, Phoenix, Arizona, 1977 - 1988
Personnel Manager, COMTEL, Columbus, Ohio, 1975 - 1977
Employee Relations Manager, UNICOM, Columbus, Ohio, 1973 - 1975
Assistant Personnel Examiner, City of Phoenix, Phoenix, Arizona, 1970 - 1973

EDUCATION

KENT STATE UNIVERSITY, Kent, Ohio, **Bachelor of Arts,** Political Science, International Relations, 1970

CYNTHIA LEE
9 Liberty Lane, Philadelphia, Pennsylvania 19122
(215) 556-XXXX

SUMMARY OF QUALIFICATIONS

Highly qualified fashion professional with a proven record in sales, training, and management. A self-motivated achiever utilizing initiative to attain goals, easily adapting to job challenges and changes.

- Excellent interpersonal, organizational, and communication skills with analytical insight in resolving complex problems.

- Possess high-level comprehension and expertise in diverse areas of marketing promotion, motivational sales training, public relations, and customer service.

- Extensive training in color analysis, make-up selection and application, personal shopping, and wardrobing.

EXPERIENCE

FASHION FOCUS INTERNATIONAL, Philadelphia, Pennsylvania, 1990 - present

PRESIDENT, 1990 - present

Established and implemented image/cosmetic business in a total concept, full-service beauty salon. Built a client base of 400+ through innovative, educational marketing techniques including fashion image/make-up seminars conducted throughout the community.

- Consistently rank in top 20 (out of 500) most productive accounts nationwide for Beauty For All Seasons. Manage all aspects of sales, training, advertising, accounting, and public relations.

- Maintain 60% repeat business through in-salon promotional activities, fliers, mailings, and image updates.

- Conduct workshops and seminars at major corporations, hospitals, and community organizations to educate on image and wardrobe.

BEAUTY FOR ALL SEASONS, Philadelphia, Pennsylvania, 1988 - 1991

REGIONAL ACCOUNT MANAGER, 1990 - 1991

Managed sell in, sell through, and counter staff training at Sears locations and independent accounts throughout Philadelphia area.

- Increased sales volume 27%. Trained and supervised in-store staff. Advised department managers on variety of marketing techniques through effective in-store promotions. Coordinated in-store promotional events including fashion shows and makeovers.

- Maintained sell through and profitability by conducting seminars and workshops and acquainting management with methodology.

- Developed workshops and trained new accounts on color theory, make-up application, product knowledge, and sales methods.

RECRUITING/TRAINING MANAGER, 1988 - 1990

Set up and managed training department with a staff of 13, handling the planning and conducting of 40 annual nationwide training seminars.

Recruited new accounts nationwide by telemarketing and in-person sales presentations. Managed two-person telemarketing department and six-person sales force.

- Increased new accounts by 126% within one year.

LIBERTY TEMPS, Philadelphia, Pennsylvania, 1986 - 1988

MARKETING REPRESENTATIVE, 1986 - 1988

Maintained top ranking as marketing representative averaging 15 new accounts weekly and doubling the company's new account average. Developed new business through cold calls, sales presentations, and effective proposals. Assisted in interviewing, hiring, and training marketing representatives.

- Interviewed and tested temporary applicants, assessed employer needs, and filled job orders. Contacted employers for follow-up to determine customer satisfaction.

- Acquired expertise in problem resolution. Assisted branch managers in identifying and successfully resolving problems.

THE GRAND SALON, Philadelphia, Pennsylvania, 1984 - 1986

SALES ASSISTANT/WOMEN'S FASHIONS, 1984 - 1986

Established and maintained extensive clientele. Assisted clients in make-up and wardrobe selection.

- Coordinated trunk shows for visiting designers. Participated in specialized training by representatives of visiting designers.

EDUCATION

TEMPLE UNIVERSITY, Philadelphia, Pennsylvania
B.A. in Political Science and minor in Broadcasting and Media Communications, 1983

PROFESSIONAL DEVELOPMENT
Numerous courses in Sales and Management, Image and Fashion Training, Recruiting and Promotion Skills

CERTIFICATION

Certified Image Consultant, Beauty For All Seasons

PROFESSIONAL ASSOCIATIONS

National Association of Female Executives
Association of Fashion and Image Consultants

Willing to Relocate

LORRAINE KAISEN, CPA, CIA

335 Glade Way
Miami, Florida 33100
Work (305) 888-XXXX Home (305) 999-XXXX

CAREER HISTORY

Extensive experience establishing and managing effective internal audit functions. Proven record in developing internal audit departments, assisting organizations in meeting their goals.

EXPERIENCE

UNIVERSITY OF MIAMI, Coral Gables, Florida

DIRECTOR OF INTERNAL AUDIT, 1987 - present

Assumed responsibility of audit department for large university not in compliance with audit standards. Developed and implemented long-range plan to restructure department; worked around major budget cuts resulting in severe limitations of staff and financial resources.

Complied with performance requirements by adopting the Institute of Internal Auditors (IIA) Standards, establishing effective policies and procedures, and hiring and training a new staff of six.

Increased department's effectiveness by upgrading computer and software and producing constructive audit reports. Provided special services to management by accessing selected data from the mainframe system and making this information available to other university departments.

NATIONAL TELEPHONE COMPANY (NTC), Miami, Florida

AUDIT MANAGER, 1985 - 1987

Independently completed five to seven operational and financial audits per year, primarily in the Chief Financial Officer's organization.

Oversaw one to two large audit projects per year, consisting of three to seven individual audits. Established scope, timing, and budgets. Recommended for promotion to District Manager.

INTERNAL AUDITOR, 1983 - 1985

Special assignment to supervise five auditors. Assessed vendor's controls over the billing (contracted out), collection, payment, and reporting of NTC's various long-distance revenue services.

SENIOR INTERNAL AUDITOR, 1980 - 1983

Performed financial and operational audits in all company areas for Business Function unit. Developed audit programs, conducted audits, wrote and issued audit reports. Consistently received highest ratings from supervisor.

SOUTHERN SYSTEMS, Atlanta, Georgia

SENIOR INTERNAL AUDITOR, 1979 - 1980

Performed in-depth operational audits covering manufacturing, financial, and sales operations for manufacturer with $80 million in annual sales.

ALBANY STATE COLLEGE, Albany, Georgia

INTERNAL AUDITOR, 1975 - 1979

Established the internal audit function at large state university. Developed the Audit Charter, long-term audit plans, and policies and procedures. Conducted financial and compliance audits in all university areas. Managed staff of two.

CRAMER, FISK & COMPANY, Atlanta, Georgia

SENIOR STAFF AUDITOR, 1972 - 1975

Progressed with local CPA firm. Conducted certified audits and provided management services.

EDUCATION

Master of Accountancy, 1973
  EMORY UNIVERSITY, Atlanta, Georgia

Bachelor of Science in Accounting, cum laude, 1971
  UNIVERSITY OF GEORGIA, Athens, Georgia

CERTIFICATIONS

Certified Public Accountant, Georgia
Certified Internal Auditor

CHARLOTTE BLOCK
7 Fisher Avenue, Eastchester, New York 10709
Work (212) 666-XXXX Home (914) 961-XXXX

HIGHLY QUALIFIED COMPUTER PROFESSIONAL

EXPERIENCE

HIGH TECHNOLOGY ASSOCIATES, New York, New York, 1989 - present

Assigned to contracted projects for the City of New York and Port Authority of New York as LAN Manager, LAN Specialist, Programmer Analyst, and Microcomputer Specialist.

Extensive knowledge of Personal Computer hardware and software support, 3Com3Share 1.6 and Microsoft LAN Manager 2.1 Local Area Networking (LAN), and Wide Area Data Networking (WADN).

♦ Plan and implement network system upgrades and handle network administration.

♦ Provide software, hardware, and communication analysis.

♦ Maintain network servers and numerous peripherals including: Repeaters, FAX Servers, Bridge/Routers/Brouters, CSUs/DSUs, scanners, modems, and printers.

♦ Research and test hardware and software packages and conduct methods and procedures analysis.

♦ Set workstation configuration standards, train individuals and groups, and develop user manuals.

INTEGRATED SOLUTIONS INC., New York, New York, 1984 - 1989

Progressive experience with computer contracting firm as Methods and Procedures Analyst, Associate Methods and Procedures Analyst, Lead Computer Operator, and Associate Computer Operator.

Acquired extensive knowledge with Harris Mini-computer software and Personal Computer hardware and software support.

♦ Conducted Personal Computer, 3Com Local Area Network, and Harris Mini-computer system (hardware and software) training and provided technical support for Port Authority employees.

♦ Researched and tested hardware and software packages for the Port Authority of New York.

♦ Developed user manuals, maintained equipment, and performed methods and procedures analysis.

INTERNATIONAL COMPUTERS, New York, New York, 1981 - 1984

As Lead Computer Operator, supervised support personnel and the operation of three Harris Mini-computers.

♦ Maintained all system peripherals including tape drives, printers, and communication equipment. Assisted users in hardware and software troubleshooting.

TECHNICAL SKILLS

Network Operating Systems

3Com 3Plus 3Share 1.6, Microsoft LAN Manager 2.1, 3Com 3+OPEN 1.0, Novell Netware 3.1

Computer Hardware

3Com 3Servers/3Server 386s/Bridges/Routers/Brouters, 3Com NETbuilder/NETbuilder II, 3Com LBR2000/LBR3000, 3Com MultiConnect Repeater, Cabletron Repeater, MMAC 8, various CSUs and DSUs, various XT/AT/Micro-Channel clones, COMPAQ 286/386/Portable II/SystemPro 486, various laptops and portables, various Laser and color printers, Microtek MSF-300C Image Scanner, Kurzeweil K5000 scanner, Harris 100/300/500/700/1000, Data General Library System

Application Software

PC/MS-DOS, OS/2, Microsoft Windows, WordPerfect, Quarterdeck Expanded Memory Manager, Qualitas 386MAX, Microsoft Word, Lotus 1-2-3, dBase III+, Crosstalk XVI, ProComm, Norton Utilities, Graphwriter II, Freelance Plus Series, Harvard Graphics, PC Paintbrush Plus, Picture It, Show Partner, Ashton Tate Graphics Series, Micrografx Designer, Adobe Illustrator, Zenographics, Ventura Publisher, Pagemaker, PC Tools, CheckIt

EDUCATION

A.A. candidate, Computer Information Systems/Systems Analysis

Westchester Community College, Valhalla, New York

HONORS/AWARDS

3Com 3Wizard Certification, 1991

Performance commendation, Port Authority of New York, 1990, 1989

Jason James
57 Cherry Blossom Court, Oakton, Virginia 22124
Home (703) 255-XXXX Work (202) 444-XXXX

QUALIFICATIONS SUMMARY

Extensive experience and expertise in energy, environment, and education issues. Thorough knowledge of Congress and how it works. Excellent writing, speaking, and problem-solving skills.

EXPERIENCE

UNITED STATES SENATE

SENIOR LEGISLATIVE ASSISTANT FOR SENATOR WORTHY, 1984 - present

Staff expert for energy, environment, and education issues. Sole responsibility for analyzing, summarizing, and recommending action to the Senator on all legislative issues.

- Acquired expertise by studying, researching, and drafting legislation; attending briefings, hearings, and seminars; communicating verbally and in writing with individuals and groups. Visited local schools and off-site programs and met with school officials and constituent groups.

- Planned several Congressional hearings, selected and briefed witnesses, and prepared statements and questions.

- Developed extensive network of contacts in Congress and the Executive Branch. Principal liaison to Department of Energy, Environmental Protection Agency, Interior Department, Federal Energy Regulatory Commission, Nuclear Regulatory Commission, and Department of Education.

- Wrote floor statements, testimony, reports, speeches, news articles, and responses to constituent correspondence.

- Made speeches and public appearances on behalf of the Senator.

- Resolved problems with the Federal government for State agencies and institutions.

LEGISLATIVE ASSISTANT FOR SENATOR HOPE, 1977 - 1984

Promoted from Special Assistant to Legislative Assistant. Researched and wrote issue papers on energy and education. Monitored Senate floor activities, attended hearings, and drafted summaries for Legislative Director.

- Edited and processed legislative correspondence to constituents and government officials. Compiled quarterly legislative reports.

- Coordinated summer intern program and supervised interns.

EDUCATION

Bachelor of Arts in English, George Mason University, Fairfax, Virginia

MADELINE VALENTINE

52 Blackstone Terrace
Salem, Oregon 97310
Work (503) 221-XXXX Home (503) 222-XXXX

CAREER SUMMARY

Resourceful manager and team player with consistent performance and progressive experience. Adept at identifying problems, developing action plans, and achieving results.

EXPERIENCE

SALEM FINANCE CORPORATION, Salem, Oregon, 1988 - present

LENDING MANAGER, 1989 - present

Plan and direct all sales activities for consumer finance organization. Develop and recommend branch budgets and sales goals. Manage sales staff: interview and hire employees, train, assign goals, monitor progress, and review performance. Perform daily audit of books, loans, and cash transactions, ensuring compliance with state and federal regulations. Handle personal portfolio of over $4 million.

Branch experienced a growth of $3.5 million from 1990 through 1993.

ASSISTANT LENDING MANAGER, 1988 - 1989

Introduced and sold consumer loans to prospective clients. Obtained leads through telemarketing, cold calling, direct mailings, and current customer base. Processed loan applications, investigated credit history, and disbursed cash amounts. Consulted clients on financial alternatives, credit options, and possible payment arrangements.

NATIONWIDE INSURANCE, Salem, Oregon, 1985 - 1987

SALES REPRESENTATIVE, 1985 - 1987

Successfully sold life insurance policies. Canvassed assigned territory, identified prospects, and utilized effective marketing techniques.

'EDUCATION/PROFESSIONAL DEVELOPMENT

PORTLAND STATE UNIVERSITY, Portland, Oregon
Bachelor of Business Administration, 1987

SALEM FINANCE CORPORATION, Salem, Oregon
Assistant Manager Training Program, Manager Qualification Program, Interactive Sales Skills Seminar, Winning Performance Through Sales Excellence Seminar

LICENSES

Oregon State Insurance License
Notary Public - State of Oregon

Résumé 49

JEFFREY K. WILSON
35 Swamp Road, Newtown, Pennsylvania 18940
(215) 444-XXXX

CAREER SUMMARY: Extensive experience as a librarian and educator in academic and public settings. Expertise in applying and utilizing computer technology to meet user needs. Strong commitment to teaching library skills, enabling users to become independent lifelong learners.

EXPERIENCE

Bucks County Public Schools

HEAD LIBRARIAN, Doylestown High School, Doylestown, Pennsylvania, 1988 - 1993

Planned and established a high school library. Instituted and implemented a collection development program. Supervised purchase and installation of CD-ROM and software.

Encouraged greater use of library; developed and taught classes in bibliographic instruction and worked one-on-one with students. Worked effectively with faculty and staff; held group and individual meetings to identify resource needs and support curriculum. Trained staff and students on CD-ROM.

LIBRARIAN, Lambertville High School, Lambertville, Pennsylvania, Summer 1988

Supervised all aspects of the library program for high school summer session.

LIBRARY MEDIA SPECIALIST, New Hope High School, New Hope, Pennsylvania, 1985 - 1987

Provided reference services through traditional and computerized sources for high school. Catalogued audiovisual and computer software materials. Taught classes in bibliographic instruction. Sole responsibility for teaching and providing on-line services (Dialog). Worked on retrospective conversion for computerized catalog and circulation system (Winnebago).

Bucks County Public Library

REFERENCE LIBRARIAN, Doylestown Public Library, Doylestown, Pennsylvania, 1980 - 1985

Delivered reference and readers advisory services for county public library. Maintained vertical file, created bibliographies, and taught patrons how to use CD-ROM technology.

City of Trenton

ENGLISH TEACHER, James Fenimore Cooper High School, Trenton, New Jersey, 1975 - 1977

Taught English literature and grammar.

EDUCATION

Master of Library Science, University of Pennsylvania, Philadelphia, Pennsylvania, 1979
Bachelor of Arts, English Literature, Minor in Education, Moravian College, Bethlehem, Pennsylvania, 1974

CERTIFICATION

Certified by Pennsylvania and New Jersey as Librarian in K - 12 and as Secondary English Teacher

PROFESSIONAL ASSOCIATIONS

American Library Association
American Association of School Librarians
Young Adult Library Services Association

ROGER CARPENTER

55 Windy Knoll, Old Westbury, New York 11568
Work (212) 888-XXXX Home (516) 777-XXXX

CAREER OBJECTIVE: A financial position in banking with increased responsibility.

EXPERIENCE

BANK OF NEW YORK, New York, New York

LOAN ACCOUNTING SUPERVISOR, 1988 - present

Perform credit analyses for commercial credit and assist with potential customers. Prepare loan closing documents for consumer and commercial loans; review documentation and monitor data entry for loan portfolio of $48 million. Compile summary loan reports for Board of Directors and Loan Officer's Committee and regulatory reports. Conduct Lotus 1-2-3 and WordPerfect training. Provide customer service to borrowers.

LOAN ACCOUNTING ASSISTANT, 1987 - 1988

Maintained loan portfolio and performed loan data input. Supervised perfection of loan documentation. Contributed to effective customer relations.

HUDSON BANK OF NEW YORK (formerly NYC BANK), New York, New York

NOTE TELLER, 1986 - 1987

Performed data entry of demand loans. Reviewed credit lines and floor plans and settled credit life accounts. Assisted borrowers.

COLLATERAL CLERK, 1985 - 1986

Perfected titles held as collateral. Settled credit life accounts.

EDUCATION

ASSOCIATE IN SCIENCE, Business Administration, 1985
Columbia-Greene Community College, Hudson, New York

PROFESSIONAL TRAINING

Fundamentals of Real Estate Appraisal, 1991
Pace University

Analyzing Financial Statement, 1990; **Improving Your Management Skills**, 1989; **Secured Loan Documentation**, 1988
American Institute of Banking

Loan Documentation and Analysis of Article 9 of the Uniform Commercial Code, 1988
New York Bankers Association

ASSOCIATIONS

Young Bankers Section of New York Bankers Association
American Institute of Banking - Bank Representative

ANNA KIM
9 Main Street
San Francisco, California 94117
Work (415) 777-XXXX, Extension 345 Home (415) 888-XXXX

BACKGROUND SUMMARY

Extensive sales and marketing experience in the fashion and cosmetic industries with a proven sales track record.

- Strong interpersonal and communications skills.

- Fluent in Japanese. Thorough knowledge of Japanese business and social customs.

- Worldwide travel experience.

EXPERIENCE

MAKE-UP ARTIST
  MACY'S, San Francisco, California, 1989 - present

Promote cosmetic sales for the Christian Dior line. Generate business by approaching customers, scheduling appointments, and demonstrating product benefits. Coordinate special events to attract clientele.

Top producer in the bay area.

COUNTER MANAGER
  NORDSTROM'S, Seattle, Washington, 1988 - 1989

Managed sales for the Estee Lauder cosmetic line and supervised two salesclerks. Created effective displays, ticketed and replenished stock. Handled inventory and placed monthly orders.

Top producer in the state.

MODEL
  JON LEONARD and SPENCER FUR, London, England, 1983 - 1986

Developed clientele and produced sales modeling clothing and furs. Successfully increased fur sales in the Japanese market. Learned to work with people of all nationalities and at all levels.

EDUCATION

Tokyo University, Tokyo, Japan, **Associate in Arts, English**, 1977

BRADLEY F. MORAN
8 Harper Lane
Hyattsville, Maryland 20780
(301) 444-XXXX

A take-charge Program Manager successfully coordinating projects from proposal through delivery.

EXPERIENCE

DEPARTMENT OF DEFENSE (DOD), Washington, D.C., 1966 - 1993

Management Analyst, Office of the Comptroller, 1984 - 1993

Developed and controlled the Agency's integrated Management Information Systems (MIS). Established the methods and procedures used in the analyzing, testing, evaluating, controlling, and operating of the DOD's central database compiled through extraction and compilation of data from the Agency's major Automated Information Systems (AISs).

Furnished technical advice, guidance, and assistance to all staff levels. Coordinated and assigned tasks to staff at Primary Level Field Activities and tested and evaluated resulting changes.

Provided knowledge and expertise ensuring that all systems efficiently, effectively, and successfully met Agency's goals.

Computer Systems Analyst, Office of Telecommunications and Information Systems, 1980 - 1984

Administered entire Automated Information Systems, from concept to implementation, for approximately 2 million items of supply with an inventory value in excess of $3 billion. Managed concept development, feasibility determination, design and development, documentation, testing, implementation, and operational continuity.

Developed and reviewed cost benefit analysis and made recommendations. Met federal requirements by formulating and evaluating plans. Generated and reviewed scheduled steps and implemented and approved actions.

Maintained state-of-the-art awareness of all areas of data processing/information. Wrote regulations, manuals, and procedures to maintain, operate, and monitor the system.

Digital Computer Systems Analyst, Administrative Support Center, 1966 - 1980

Designed, implemented, and completed analysis of broad and complex ADP systems in support of headquarters. Supported three major functional areas as a functional ADP expert specialist. Provided systems analysis and support to other Federal agencies and departments. Conducted systematic studies of functional work processes including feasibility analysis and economic evaluation of alternate approaches.

FEDERAL HOUSING ADMINISTRATION, Washington, D. C., 1963 - 1966

Systems Analyst and Digital Computer Programmer, 1963 - 1966

Developed a complete operating system, from concept to implementation.

EDUCATION

Bachelor of Science in Business Administration, 1959
Michigan State University, East Lansing, Michigan

HARDWARE

IBM 1401, 1410, 7074, S360/20, S360/30, S370/155

CDC 915, Calcomp Plotter & Micro-film Machine

AMDAHL V7/V8

TANDEM

SOFTWARE

360 TOS/DOS COBOL, 1410 OS, 360 Linear Programming, Structured Programming, DBMS, ENABLE, WordStar, WordSoft, Lotus 1-2-3, Microsoft Windows, SQL

Top Secret Security Clearance

TONY FORTUNE

76 Grand Avenue
Dallas, Texas 75246
Work (214) 888-XXXX Home (214) 222-XXXX

Career Objective: A leadership role in management and organizational development improving the internal capability to respond to strategic challenges driven by customer and business requirements.

PROFILE

Over 15 years demonstrated success in Organizational Development, Management Development, Human Resource Management, Training, and Consulting Services.

EXPERIENCE AND RESULTS

Manager, Management and Organization Development, 1990 - present
ABC TECHNOLOGY, Dallas, Texas

Lead and guide business units in the strategic planning, design, development, implementation, and evaluation of core systems, practices, and curriculum.

- Established company-wide team and individual development planning system including process, tools, curriculum, train the trainer, and certification methodology.

- Designed, developed, and delivered line and mid-management training, institutes, and organization improvement programs for client groups. Internal demand for products and tools up 75%. Training replicated company-wide.

- Directed task force initiative to institute company-wide comprehensive electronic training tracking system.

- Led cross operational task force to design and institute company-wide PC-based development planning and organization information software system. 75% of business units are pursuing access.

- Selected to consult/advise the program management council on the plan, design, development, implementation, and evaluation of program management quality improvement initiatives.

- Established and led cross organization team in the design and pilot of a development center concept. Centers will double in one year due to favorable response.

- Designed and implemented first company-wide orientation/assimilation process including facilitator guide and employee information guides.

Principal HRD Specialist, 1985 - 1990
XYZ ELECTRONICS, Houston, Texas

Led region in the strategic planning, design, development, implementation, and evaluation of core systems, practices, and curriculum.

- Initiated, developed, and facilitated the annual strategic planning and team development offsite for executive management.

- Directed regional implementation of employee surveys, performance management system, succession planning, high-potential programming, and regional development planning.

- Designed and delivered various training and development programs and curriculum in change management, cross-functional team development, performance improvement, and management and leadership assessment methodology.

Independent HR Consultant, 1981 - 1985

Provided consulting services in cross-agency program planning, business planning, team development, instructional design, and curriculum development to private and public sector clients.

County Resource Specialist, 1976 - 1983
LOS ANGELES COUNTY, Los Angeles, California

Piloted liaison role between Los Angeles County Board of Education and special educators, providing a full range of staff development services.

EDUCATION

M.A., Counseling Psychology, Rice University, Houston, Texas, 1982

B.S., Education, Pepperdine University, Malibu, California, 1975

HONORS/AWARDS

ABC Technology Award for Outstanding Performance, 1991
XYZ Electronics Superior Performance Awards, 1989, 1988
XYZ Electronics Award for Outstanding Achievement, 1986

PROFESSIONAL AFFILIATIONS

American Society for Training and Development
National Social Sciences Honor Society

PAMELA KIDDER

99 University Way
Philadelphia, Pennsylvania 19140
Work (215) 555-XXXX Home (215) 556-XXXX

QUALIFICATION SUMMARY

Broad range of progressive experience in the temporary services industry. Highly successful in developing and establishing new business in the health care community.

EXPERIENCE

BRANCH MANAGER, 1990 - present
LIBERTY TEMPORARY SERVICES, Philadelphia, Pennsylvania

Direct sales/operations of a temporary help service providing quality temporary nurses staffing all major Philadelphia-area hospitals. Market services, develop and maintain client base, interview and place nurses.

BRANCH MANAGER, 1986 - 1990
HEALTH CARE PERSONNEL POOL, Pittsburgh, Pennsylvania

Directed sales and operations of branch and satellite offices of the oldest and largest provider of home health care and supplemental staffing in the U.S.A. Generated 30% increase in branch sales.

Set up pay/bill rates; hired, developed and conducted training; solved problems and coordinated public relations. Supervised EDPPR/Billing system, accounts payable, accounts receivable, and credit and collections.

PRESIDENT, 1980 - 1985
COMPANY NURSE, INC. (CNI), Cherry Hill, New Jersey

Established business providing temporary nursing staff for Occupational Health programs and successfully marketed programs to individuals or groups of health care providers. Staffed and managed health care services at work site, established health promotion and health education programs, and provided temporary staffing.

CHARGE NURSE, 1975 - 1978
SHETLAND HOSPITAL, Cherry Hill, New Jersey

Performed staff scheduling, patient assignments, and patient care in Neonatal Intensive Care Unit. Handled nursing responsibilities. Functioned as Head Nurse and Supervisor in staff supervisor's absence.

REGISTERED NURSE, 1971 - 1974
LIBERTY HOSPITAL, Philadelphia, Pennsylvania

Administered nursing care for medical/surgical intensive care and pediatric patients. Assisted in air transport of adult medical/surgical patients. Functioned as team leader in home care setting.

EDUCATION

Bachelor of Science, Nursing with specialty in Administration and Pediatrics, 1970
BISHOP HOSPITAL SCHOOL OF NURSING, Pittsburgh, Pennsylvania

LICENSES

Registered Nurse - Pennsylvania, New Jersey

CASEY COLLINS

843 Rose Court, Mahopac, New York 10541 (914) 933-XXXX

CAREER SUMMARY

- Progressive promotions to increased responsibility in the telecommunications industry.
- Expertise in voice and data communication sales. Highly skilled in identifying revenue opportunities, prioritizing accounts, analyzing customer requirements, developing account plans, persevering, overcoming objections, and successfully closing sales.
- Extensive experience delivering face-to-face and group presentations and utilizing effective communication skills. Excellent interpersonal skills and the ability to build solid business relationships.

EXPERIENCE

NEW YORK TELEPHONE

Senior Account Executive, New York, New York, 1988 - 1993

Provided full-service account management and marketed a diverse line of voice and data network services and customer premise equipment (CPE) to 35 major accounts in the education market in Putnam County.

- Consistently achieved 200% of sales objectives; successfully identified customers' business needs and provided solutions with New York Telephone products and services.
- Recognized as industry expert. Contributed to the development of application packages for the education market. Identified education market needs/requirements and provided integrated system solutions.
- Managed territory revenue base and all account activity resulting in increased market share. Developed account and sales plans, directed efforts of sales team, oversaw system implementations, and ensured overall customer satisfaction.

Account Representative, Yonkers, New York, 1986 - 1987

Sold directory advertising to cross-industry accounts. Protected revenue base and increased business. Adhered to linear flow guidelines and completed all campaigns on schedule.

- Increased revenue of assigned accounts by 25% - 30%.

NATIONAL OFFICE SYSTEMS, INC.

Staff Assistant, Armonk, New York, 1980 - 1982

Managed facilities for 50-person sales organization including a telecommunications system. Coordinated nationwide trade shows.

- Successfully coordinated the branch's relocation from Boston to Armonk. Completed move on schedule and under allocated budget.

ADVANTAGE SPORTSWEAR

Sales Representative, New York, New York, 1978 - 1979

Sold women's ready-to-wear. Established and maintained accounts with specialty and department stores in four-state area.

- Increased sales revenue by 25%. Opened 22 new accounts including 3 major department stores.

EDUCATION

B.S. Business Administration, Marymount College, Tarrytown, New York, 1978

SUZANNE SNYDER

15 Wiehle Avenue, Reston, Virginia 22090 Work (703) 437-XXXX Home (703) 436-XXXX

SUMMARY OF QUALIFICATIONS

Extensive experience organizing and managing all aspects of meetings and conventions including workshops, symposia, and exhibitions for organizations in the public and private sectors.

- ◆ Establish and implement conference and meeting services. Assist with the design and format of a meeting, define the agenda and attendance, select and negotiate the site, and invite speakers and presenters.

- ◆ Coordinate and organize volunteer help, process registrations, design and develop promotional and program materials, and recruit and supervise staff.

- ◆ Handle budget development and financial management, on-site supervision and logistical management.

EXPERIENCE

MEETINGS MANAGER, 1991 - present
Snyder & Associates, Reston, Virginia

Plan, manage, and coordinate all factors of meeting planning for a variety of clients. Provide services in budget development and financial management, on-site supervision, and logistical management.

- ◆ Conducted on-site management for a series of 4 seminars for 150 attendees sponsored by a major oil company.

- ◆ Coordinated logistics and registration procedures for a 6-month series of training courses for 1,100 employees of a large federal government contractor.

- ◆ Managed a fee-paid technical conference for 200 attendees sponsored by a major software company.

CONVENTION MANAGER, 1987 - 1990
American Association of Manufacturers, Reston, Virginia

Established convention services department. Planned, developed, and executed all pre-convention, on-site, and post-convention activities, and logistics for annual convention of 1,200 attendees.

- ◆ Assisted in educational programming for the convention; reviewed proposals and selected presenters.

- ◆ Negotiated and managed airline travel for staff, officers, and convention participants.

MEETINGS MANAGER, 1982 - 1986
American Society of Managers, Washington, D.C.

Planned, promoted, and managed annual meeting attended by over 2,400 participants including exhibitions, workshops, Board of Directors' meetings, and committee meetings.

- ◆ Managed all functions of 75 booth exhibitions.

EDUCATION

American Society of Association Executives: "Effective Convention Management"

Meeting Planners International: "Meeting Management"

The George Washington University: Liberal Arts Education

HARRIS WAVERLY
99 Mason Street, Hattiesburg, Mississippi 39402
(601) 222-XXXX

Career Objective: A management position with a large hotel-motel.

EXPERIENCE

GENERAL MANAGER, 1990 - present
DAYS INN, Hattiesburg, Mississippi

Oversee all aspects of running large (125 units) motel. Supervise maintenance, housekeeping, and front desk. Manage staff of 45; interview, hire, train, and evaluate performance.

- Prepare and administer budgets, handle large volumes of cash and credit card transactions, and make bank deposits. Prepare daily, weekly, and monthly reports dealing with housekeepers' minutes per room (M.P.R.), inventory costs per room, occupancy revenue, and Average Daily Rate (A.D.R.).

- Administer and audit all procedures of front desk, phone system, and reservations. Keep inventory and order supplies. Handle guests inquiries and concerns.

- Conduct surveys of the competition for prices, amenities, and employment opportunities.

NIGHT MANAGER, 1987 - 1990
GUEST SERVICE REPRESENTATIVE, 1983 - 1987
SOUTHERN INN, Biloxi, Mississippi

Progressive promotions and increased responsibility at a business-oriented hotel. Consistently met/exceeded the needs and requirements of guests. Performed beyond job expectations to satisfy guest needs.

- Adeptly utilized computer system to register guests and reserve rooms. Provided hotel information and assisted guests with multitude of local information.

- Processed payments and posted charges to guest accounts, ensuring accounts balanced on a daily basis.

- Effectively and efficiently resolved guest problems and complaints.

- Trained new employees on computer system and customer relations.

EDUCATION

Professional Development: Days Inn Management School, Southern Inn Management School

East Central Community College, Decatur, Mississippi: Course work toward degree in Hotel Management

LOUISE JACKSON

9 Elm Street, Chicago, Illinois 60600
(312) 424-XXXX

CAREER OBJECTIVE

A position as a registered nurse in an occupational, clinical, or hospital setting.

EXPERIENCE

STAFF NURSE
   City Hospital, Chicago, Illinois, 1992 - 1993

Assumed responsibilities of charge nurse and staff nurse. Oversaw patient care; communicated with physician concerning patient needs, assessed patient requirements, made assignments, and delegated responsibilities to staff members. Ensured quality care by providing clear, concise, intershift communications and accurately documenting patient care.

Utilized the nursing process with individuals and groups and participated in treatment planning. Initiated problem-solving strategies with co-workers to facilitate quality patient outcomes. Administered medications, coordinated lab work and treatments according to institute's policies and procedures.

REGISTERED NURSE/STAFF NURSE
   Doctor's Hospital, Chicago, Illinois, 1987 - 1992

Worked in acute care setting as primary care nurse with responsibility for ten acute patients. Provided immediate post-op care as ordered by physician; administered medications, I.V. infusions, and blood transfusions. Conducted family/patient teaching prior to discharge. Performed admission process for patients admitted through emergency room.

HOME CARE INDEPENDENT CONTRACTOR
   Chicago, Illinois, 1986

Scheduled home care visits and provided nursing care to patients recovering from cancer, bypass, and abdominal surgeries. Assessed patients and recommended community resources.

STAFF NURSE
   General Hospital, Peoria, Illinois, 1982 - 1985

Administered nursing care for 28 medical and surgical patients. Handled admitting process and provided quality nursing care. Assumed charge nurse responsibility for 3-11 shift.

LICENSES

Registered Nurse - State of Illinois

EDUCATION

Bachelor of Science in Nursing, University of Chicago, Chicago, Illinois, 1981
Professional Development: Attended numerous seminars/courses for career development

FRANCINE GIOVANONI
90 Mountain View
San Luis Obispo, California 93401
(805) 999-XXXX

QUALIFICATIONS SUMMARY

Senior member of Medical Service Corps Exec Team with management background in health care delivery systems and organizational responsibility of up to 100 people.

- Highly successful in motivating staff to achieve organizational goals while providing optimal customer care.

- Recognized specialist in managing multiple and diverse assignments, handling patient crises, interdepartmental conflicts, and abrasive personalities with finesse.

EXPERIENCE

Senior Nursing Supervisor, 1992 - present
    VANDENBERG MEDICAL CENTER, Vandenberg AFB, California

Manage and supervise nursing activities of a 235-bed Medical Center. Oversee and provide administrative support for emergency room and 12 inpatient units. Supervise 25 RN's and 50 paraprofessionals.

- Instruct, guide, and consult with personnel in matters of patient and administrative issues and clinical problems. Represent Chief Nurse during after-hours.

Chief Nurse, 1988 - 1992
    DAVID GRANT USAF MEDICAL CENTER, Travis AFB, California

Planned, supervised, and evaluated the activities of 3 full-time registered nurses (RN), 33 medical service technicians, and 5 Individual Mobilization Augmentees RNs.

Assigned personnel to job positions, maintained care continuity. Initiated, implemented, and maintained education programs promoting staff knowledge, skill, and career development.

- Developed best trained nursing staff in Air Force (AF), exceeding AF standards with certification in Emergency Medical Technician (EMT), advanced cardiac life support, and EMT Intermediate.

- Used cases from literature to improve adequacy of patient education. Increased teaching documentation from 35% professional staff compliance to 100% in Primary Care/Family Practice.

- Led in Total Quality Management improvement initiatives. Educated people, initiated journal club, and forwarded synopsis of paradigms to 200 members through computer mail.

- Obtained affiliate faculty status for Basic Cardiac Life Support program for entire facility, saving innumerable hours spent under actual instruction/supervision and commuting to oversight facility.

- Imaginatively approached and skillfully coordinated the annual Health Fair and turned it into an impressive display of Tri-Service military health care serving over 500 people. Organized extensive hypertensive screening of over 420 people on 2 bases and identified 66 individuals for follow-up.

Surgical Nursing Coordinator, 1983 - 1988
15TH MEDICAL GROUP, Hickam AFB, Hawaii

Progressive promotions from Assistant Charge Nurse to Surgical Nursing Coordinator. Planned, supervised, evaluated, and organized nursing care in the 9-bed Intensive Care Unit, a 36-bed Male Surgical Unit, and a 44-bed Female Surgical Unit.

- Supervised 40 nurses and 40 technicians; evaluated performance, counseled, and coordinated staff development. Efficiently handled complex unit management and patient care decisions. Assisted in determining manning requirements, recommended key personnel for job positions, and redistributed personnel according to criticality of individual unit needs.

- Maximized staffing. Suggested a call system for critical care units to enhance bed use and patient access. Eliminated waste and duplication; slashed drug inventory by 50%.

Charge Nurse/Assistant Charge Nurse, 1978 - 1983

Successfully handled Charge Nurse responsibilities and developed leadership abilities at hospitals in Alabama and Texas.

Staff Nurse, 1973 - 1978
EDWARDS MEDICAL CENTER, Edwards AFB, California

Officer-in-Charge of Operating Room Technician Program. Circulating nurse for all services except Open Heart.

- Supervised patient care in operating room. Direct responsibility for training and supervising corpsmen in Operating Room Technician Program - approximately 60 corpsmen and women at any one time.

EDUCATION

M.S. in Health Systems, 1987, University of Hawaii at Manoa, Honolulu, Hawaii

B.S. in Nursing, 1971, Emory University, Atlanta, Georgia

Service Schools: Air Command and Staff College, 1988, Instructor Training, 1977

LICENSES

R.N. - State of Georgia

PROFESSIONAL ORGANIZATIONS

American Nurses Association
American Academy of Ambulatory Nursing Administration

HONORS/AWARDS

Certification in Nursing Administration, 1991 - 1995; Awarded Chief Nurse Insignia, June 1987
Meritorious Service Medal and First Oak Leaf Cluster; Air Force Commendation Medal

THERESA ROMANO

87 East Fayette Street, Syracuse, New York 13200
Work (315) 777-XXXX Home (315) 666-XXXX

Energetic, results-oriented personnel employment professional with corporate and temporary help industry experience.

EXPERIENCE

TEMPS INC.

OFFICE MANAGER, 1988 - present
Syracuse, New York

Assumed leadership of temporary placement branch office after a complete staff turnover. Hired, trained, and supervised a staff of six. Oversaw all temporary recruitment and created promotional strategies to increase business; designed, placed, and monitored advertising; implemented strategies to ensure client satisfaction and repeat business. Created forms to track placements and profits.

Increased billable hours 25% per week and gross profits 21% per week. Increased margins and overall mark-up.

YOUR TEMP SOLUTION

SERVICE COORDINATOR, 1985 - 1988
Syracuse, New York

Interviewed, evaluated, and placed temporary clerical personnel. Maintained high level of client satisfaction. Increased repeat business by 15%.

MARKETING REPRESENTATIVE, 1983 - 1985
Rochester, New York

Utilized telemarketing and sales strategies to prospect new accounts and service existing accounts. Created promotional strategy and cultivated new clients by providing speakers to associations and non-profit organizations.

NATIONAL SECURITY SYSTEMS

RECRUITING ASSISTANT, 1976 - 1982
Rochester, New York

Promoted from Administrative Assistant after successfully handling Recruiting Assistant responsibilities for six weeks. Scheduled and coordinated interviews. Provided administrative support. Created and maintained a candidate tracking system.

EDUCATION

Course work in business management
SYRACUSE UNIVERSITY, Syracuse, New York

Associate in Arts, 1976
MONROE COMMUNITY COLLEGE, Rochester, New York

GAIL W. REED

100 Hilldale Place
San Jose, California 95153
(408) 222-XXXX

Innovative and mature church professional with broad ecumenical experience in pastoral counseling, cross-cultural understanding, program developing, and religious education.

EDUCATION

Master of Divinity, 1990
Faith Theological Seminary, San Jose, California

Bachelor of Arts, cum laude, 1972
Trinity College, Hartford, Connecticut

PROFESSIONAL TRAINING

Interim Director of Christian Education, Thomas Presbyterian Church, September - December 1989.

Seminary Intern, Mission Presbyterian Church, October 1988 - August 1989. Fulfilled seminary field education assignment.

Development Committee Member, San Jose Pastoral Counseling Service, 1989.

EXPERIENCE

PASTOR, 1991 - present
Baptist World Alliance, San Jose, California

Conduct pastoral counseling and plan programs. Retreat Leader for several churches in the San Jose area.

Wrote adult education curriculum for Northwest Yearly Meeting of Friends Churches (Quaker).

PASTORAL COUNSELOR/EDUCATION COORDINATOR, 1987 - 1988
Tokyo Union Church, Tokyo, Japan

Led retreats, workshops; developed and coordinated adult education program; taught adult education classes; assisted church school as resource person. Conducted pastoral counseling for both English-speaking and Japanese individuals. Served as requested in pastoral role with senior and assistant pastors.

INTERIM PASTOR, 1987
San Gabriel Union Church, San Jose, California

Served as the interim pastor from February - August while awaiting permanent pastor couple, at the request of the church board. Tasks involved preaching, counseling, teaching, developing Christian education for children and youth, worship planning, newsletter, publicity, and planning for new pastors.

ASSISTANT FOR PASTORAL CARE, OFFICE OF THE CHAPLAIN, 1979 - 1981
Berlin Military Chapel, Berlin, Germany

Assisted in developing and coordinating visitation program for incoming English-speaking personnel for the purposes of explaining community-wide services, counseling programs, day care, hospitals, and support groups. Supervised counseling and referrals.

RELATED EXPERIENCE

OFFICE MANAGER, 1976 - 1978
PMB, Inc., San Jose, California

Managed office for governmental consulting firm of 100 employees. Handled internal administrative operation; coordinated proposals, reports; supervised editing, layout, and proofreading. Interviewed, hired, and supervised support staff. Conducted orientation for professional staff. Maintained affirmative action and insurance benefit program.

EDITOR/WRITER, 1974 - 1976
Environmental Impact, Washington, D.C.

Editor of *Environmental Comment*, a 16-page monthly publication concerning environmental land use issues. Marketed and edited selected publications and periodicals including public relations, news releases, and promotional efforts. Monitored selected legislative issues relating to land use and housing/development industry.

ASSISTANT DIRECTOR, HEAD TEACHER, 1972 - 1973
Friends Daycare, Washington, D.C.

Assisted in forming and implementing a new day care center for 75 children. Coordinated daily program schedules, supervised staff, maintained parent visitation program. Worked with 4-C government-funded program in meeting and maintaining regulations and in planning curriculum.

DENOMINATION: Ecumenical Perspective. Minister ordained in Northwest Yearly Meeting of Friends (Quaker)

FLORENCE ZIMMERMAN
87 Forrest Avenue
Knoxville, Tennessee 37922
Work (615) 666-XXXX Home (615) 333-XXXX

EXPERIENCED COMPUTER SYSTEMS MANAGER

WORK HISTORY

CITY OF KNOXVILLE, Knoxville, Tennessee, 1982 - present

Personal Computer Manager, 1989 - present
Park and Recreation Department

Perform as PC Manager in the Information Systems and Services section. Plan and direct on-going program automating the department from 7 PCs to 32. Maintain equipment in all 6 divisions.

Assess computer needs and problems for six divisions; perform extensive investigations and communications; make computer recommendations. Plan and coordinate the placement of all computer equipment, peripherals, cabling, and electrical requirements.

Communicate and coordinate with vendors on purchases and support. Install all software and hardware. Evaluate specialized software packages and make purchase recommendations. Design programs as needed for all divisions. Train employees on departmental software programs.

Direct the polling/downloading of police incident reports using a micro/mainframe link. Coordinate and develop statistical information and reports for the departmental budget. Perform as department E-mail administrator and instructor.

Accomplishments

- Coordinated the installation of 25 personal computers.

- Oversaw the automation of the Knoxville Zoo and City's six golf courses. Investigated and analyzed information and made recommendations for purchase and installation of all computer equipment and point-of-sale programs.

- Performed daily polling/downloading of all zoo animal information and created record-keeping formats and reports.

- Supervised implementation of department's Teknicad mapping system, desktop publishing system, and project tracking/scheduling program.

PC Network Manager, 1982 - 1989
Transportation and Public Works/Engineering

Installed, maintained, and provided user support for Novell network and software. Evaluated, analyzed, and advised management on all department hardware and software requirements. Interfaced with vendor representatives.

Promoted from secretary supporting a staff of ten. Performed administrative duties; created and maintained monthly statistical reports, coordinated meetings, typed correspondence and reports using word processing software. Evaluated public requests and concerns and forwarded them to appropriate engineer.

Accomplishments

- Assisted in developing and maintaining a project tracking system designed to assist engineers in monitoring community facilities agreements.

Administrative Clerk, 1982
Purchasing Department

Prepared and released bid packages to city vendors. Coordinated vendor meetings and prepared Mayor and Council communications regarding the sale and purchase of materials and services requiring City Council approval.

WILSON & THOMAS, ATTORNEYS-AT-LAW, Knoxville, Tennessee, 1973 - 1976

Administrative Assistant, 1973 - 1976

Typed legal documents and correspondence. Handled dictation, filing, bookkeeping, and mail.

EDUCATION

Professional Development
Numerous courses in computer operations, hardware, and software

Associate in Science, Secretarial Science, 1973
Cleveland State Community College, Cleveland, Tennessee

HELEN TROY-HILL

14 Seaside Road
Portland, Maine 04103
Work (207) 889-XXXX   Home (207) 888-XXXX

BACKGROUND SUMMARY

More than 20 years' experience in office management with expertise in human resource management, business administration, and installation, administration, and training in automated office systems. Possess strong communication skills in coordinating with management, support staff, and field personnel.

TECHNICAL SKILLS

Hardware: DBS 16 (minicomputer), IBM PC/XT, IBM PC/AT

Software: WordPerfect, Lotus 1-2-3, SuperCalc2, MS-DOS

EXPERIENCE

PERSONNEL AND BENEFITS ADMINISTRATOR, 1991 - present

New England Office Systems, Portland, Maine

Administer and implement corporate benefits program. Utilize expertise in benefits and health care delivery systems to counsel employees, resolve problems, conflicts, and appeals. Process insurance enrollments, conversions, terminations, 401(k) pension plan, COBRA, and workers compensation. Track and analyze benefits costs. Prepare a variety of personnel and compliance reports for 250 employees.

Manage staff: hire, train, motivate, counsel, and review performance. Ensure payroll is prepared, processed, and distributed.

- Set up human resource function.
- Initiated and implemented personnel policies and procedures.

OFFICE MANAGER, 1987 - 1990

Liberty Mortgage Corporation, Portland, Maine

Served as liaison between the administrative and commercial mortgage offices. Disseminated various reports between the offices and established an open line of communication between production personnel and support staff. Managed secretarial staff: hired and trained staff for both the Bangor and Portland offices. Created, re-organized, and streamlined filing systems and office procedures to keep pace with increasing levels of production.

- Coordinated the move of the entire Bangor operation to new facilities, including the successful implementation of a new computerized telephone system.
- Assisted in coordinating the opening of the Portland office.
- Established standards for daily use of computer hardware and software, including an effective backup system for computer files and disks.

ASSISTANT OFFICE MANAGER, 1984 - 1987

Innovative Systems, Inc., Bangor, Maine

Instituted innovative office procedures to streamline the flow of interdepartmental business. Managed a DBS 16 minicomputer with five terminals. Resolved systems problems and trained office personnel and managerial staff in computer use. Generated weekly and monthly reports for accounts receivable, labor job cost control, wage control, and vendor information reports with SuperCalc2. Used DBS 16 computer system's accounting program to evaluate billing information and track general job-cost and job budgets and control payables.

INDEPENDENT CONSULTANT, 1980 - 1983

Assisted in the day-to-day administrative operations for a manufacturer's representative for building materials.

OFFICE MANAGER, 1970 - 1980

The Sea Shop, Portland, Maine

Increased sales by establishing innovative merchandising and advertising programs. Prepared bookkeeping reports: accounts receivable, accounts payable, and payroll.

EDUCATION

The Computer Institute, Bangor, Maine, 1984
  Diploma with distinction, in computer programming

Course work at South Main Technical College, South Portland, Maine and Community College of Vermont, Waterbury, Vermont

SUE ELLEN SHAW

88 Marley Lane
Winston-Salem, North Carolina 27108
Work (919) 811-XXXX Home (919) 811-XXXX

BACKGROUND SUMMARY: An innovative, organized **Personnel Generalist** with strong interpersonal and communication skills. Promoted three times to increasingly responsible positions.

- Exceptional problem-solving skills.
- Ability to work with all staff levels.
- Top Secret access.

CAREER OBJECTIVE

A Personnel Generalist position with a progressive, people-oriented organization.

EXPERIENCE

Southern Systems, Winston-Salem, North Carolina, 1983 - present

PERSONNEL ADMINISTRATOR, 1987 - present

Establish and maintain corporate pay system. Conduct annual salary surveys ensuring fair and equitable pay rates and compliance with Federal and state laws and regulations. Design and administer flexible corporate benefits programs. Manage a staff of four: hire, train, motivate, counsel, and review performance.

Oversee payroll process and distribution. Monitor personnel activity and reporting for 630 employees.

Plan and direct annual update of Code of Conduct, bond drive, and Shift Roster. Coordinate Employee Assistance Program (EAP) and comply with Government Statement of Work (SOW).

- Administer annual merit budget of $20 million. Coordinate all interim promotions.
- Work with Lotus 1-2-3, Multimate, dBase, and WordPerfect.
- Designed Performance Appraisal and additional tracking systems to ensure deadlines are met.

EMPLOYEE RELATIONS REPRESENTATIVE, 1985 - 1987

Developed expertise in designing and administering benefits programs. Assisted employees with complex benefits options in choosing personal coverage.

Supervised day-to-day operation of office with a staff of four.

- Coordinated housing for temporarily assigned employees.

- Arranged leases for apartments and townhouses, furnished units, and assigned employees to housing.

- Provided on-going maintenance, paid bills, and re-assigned units.

SENIOR SECRETARY, 1983 - 1985

Performed administrative and secretarial duties for the Chief of Administration. Attended meetings and kept minutes. Composed memos, provided counsel, and assisted supervisor in handling departmental responsibilities.

- Implemented a housing program for temporarily assigned workers.

- Learned security procedures and the technical aspects of the department.

High Tech, Inc., Winston-Salem, North Carolina, 1980 - 1983

ADMINISTRATIVE ASSISTANT, 1980 - 1983

Supported Regional Controller and three managers. Organized meetings, created and maintained filing systems. Provided input regarding policies for office management.

EDUCATION

Bachelor of Arts, Sociology
Charleston Southern University, Charleston, South Carolina

BELINDA BANKS, R.P.T.

78 Level Lane
Wichita, Kansas 67213
(316) 888-XXXX

EXPERIENCED PHYSICAL THERAPIST

Extensive experience administering physical therapy treatments, specializing in geriatric and home bound patients.

EXPERIENCE

Physical Therapist, 1989 - present
PT Associates of Wichita, Wichita, Kansas

Evaluate, develop, and provide treatment programs for geriatric home bound patients. Educate patients and their families.

Teach weekly physical therapy exercise class for patients with Parkinson's and recovering from stroke. Frequent lecturer for community and non-profit groups on benefits of exercise.

Staff Physical Therapist, 1989
Wichita Hospital, Wichita, Kansas

Administered physical therapy treatments. Substituted for the Director of Rehabilitation Medicine Department for five weeks. Instructor of "Back School."

Substitute Staff Physical Therapist, 1981 - 1982
Wichita Hospital, Wichita, Kansas

Provided staff coverage and treated patients in orthopedic and acute care.

Senior Physical Therapist, 1977 - 1980
Lincoln Psychiatric Center, Lincoln, Nebraska

Consulted with physician specialists in formulating physical therapy evaluations and treatment plans. Supervised four physical therapy assistants, three aides, and a secretary.

EDUCATION

Certificate in Physical Therapy, Kansas State University, Medical College, School of Physical Therapy, Manhattan, Kansas, 1971

Bachelor of Science, University of Kansas, Lawrence, Kansas, 1970

DANIEL K. AVRAM, M.D.

Curriculum Vitae

6443 Lucket Lane
Brier, Washington 98036
(206) 923-XXXX

EDUCATION

UNITED STATES INTERNATIONAL UNIVERSITY, Nairobi, Kenya
Graduate course in Family Therapy, September - December 1989

UNIVERSITY OF CALIFORNIA, Song Brown Fellowship Program, Modesto, California
Family Practice Fellow, October 1983 - 1984

MODESTO GENERAL HOSPITAL, Modesto, California
Family Practice Residency, June 1980 - 1983

UNIVERSITY OF WASHINGTON SCHOOL OF MEDICINE, Seattle, Washington
Doctor of Medicine (M.D.), June 1979

WHITMAN COLLEGE, Walla Walla, Washington
Bachelor of Arts, Biology, 1974

WORK HISTORY

FAMILY PRACTICE

Brier Family Practice, 1990 - present
Partner in large, single specialty family practice corporation in the northern Seattle area.

Locum Tenes in Family Medicine, 1986 - 1989
Locum work with five private family medicine practices in California and Washington states, and one private practice in Nairobi, Kenya.

John Lynam, M.D., Inc., 1983 - 1985
Private medical practice in Patterson, California, a predominantly Mexican and Mexican-American rural community.

Modesto General Hospital, 1983 - 1985
Private medical practice in Modesto, California.

Tabasco State Rural Health Program, 1979 - 1980
Physician in traveling village health clinic in Villahermosa, Mexico.

EMERGENCY MEDICINE

Locum Tenens in Emergency Medicine, 1987 - 1989
Emergency room physician at County Trauma Center, Modesto General Hospital, Modesto, California and Del Puerto Hospital, Patterson, California.

Emergency Care, 1987 - 1990
Physician on call for tourist, film, and mountain climbing groups visiting remote areas of East Africa.

Nairobi Hospital, 1986 - 1987
Emergency room physician, Nairobi, Kenya.

Manteca Hospital, 1983 - 1985
Emergency room physician, Manteca, California.

RESEARCH

African Medical Research and Education Foundation (AMREF), Nairobi, Kenya
Consultant, 1990

Developed questionnaire for study on malaria treatment and outcome at Nairobi Hospital.

Aga Khan Hospital, Nairobi, Kenya
Departmental Evaluator, 1987

Evaluated flow patterns and frequency of diagnosis of emergency room facilities.

Area Health Education Center, State of California
Principal Investigator, 1983 - 1985

Evaluated nutrition knowledge and training of family physicians in California.

Modesto General Hospital, Modesto, California
Member of Steering Committee for Medical Research, 1984 - 1985

TEACHING AND CURRICULUM DEVELOPMENT

Davis Free Community Clinic, Davis, California
Preceptor of medical students, 1990 - 1992

University of California, Davis, Davis, California
Assistant Clinical Professor, School of Medicine, Department of Family Practice, 1990 - 1992

Supervised and taught clinical skills to medical students and family practice residents during family practice clinical rotations.

African Medical Research and Education Foundation (AMREF), Nairobi, Kenya
Consultant, 1987 - 1990

Designed curriculum, taught clinical skills, and provided field supervision for community health care workers and planners from East Africa.

Modesto General Hospital, Modesto, California
Preceptor, 1983 - 1985

Primary clinical supervisor for physician assistant program and teaching of family practice medical residents.

Area Health Education Center, Modesto, California
Research Fellow, 1983 - 1985

Developed nutrition curriculum for California residency programs in family medicine. Clinical training of residents at Modesto General Hospital. Didactic and clinical training of physician assistants and nurse practitioners.

HONORS AND AWARDS

Song-Brown Commission Fellowship, State of California, 1983 - 1984
Diplomate, American Academy of Family Physicians, 1983 - 1990; Recertified, 1989 - 1996
Chief Resident, Modesto General Hospital, Modesto, California, 1982 - 1983

PROFESSIONAL AFFILIATIONS

American Academy of Family Practice, 1981 - present
United Health Medical Group, Inc.(Independent Physician Association for Davis Area), Member,
Board of Directors, 1991 - 1992
Sutter-Davis Hospital, Davis, California, Member, Active Staff, 1990 - present
Woodland Memorial Hospital, Woodland, California, Member, Courtesy Staff, 1990 - present
Kenya Medical Association, 1986 - 1989
American Medical Association, 1978 - 1985
California Coastal Research Groups, 1983 - 1985
Stanislaus County Child and Infant Care Association, Inc., Member, Board of Directors, 1983 - 1985
National Coalition Against Health Fraud, 1983 - 1985

LANGUAGES

English, native; Spanish, fluent; Swahili, conversational.

SELECTED PAPERS AND PUBLICATIONS

"Hidden Agendas in Patient Care."
Invited lecture presented to the University of Davis Pre-Medical Society, Davis, California, May 1991.

"Retrospective Review of Emergency Room Patient Flow Patterns and Frequency of Diagnosis."
Analysis and recommendations for the Aga Khan Hospital, Nairobi, Kenya, June 1987.

Avram, D.K., Gossel, C., Welsher, J.
"Nutrition Education for Family Practice Residents," *Journal of Family Medicine*, 1:837-39, 1985.

"Teaching and Learning Outpatient Nutrition."
Teaching Seminar presented at the Society of Teachers of Family Medicine Annual Meeting, Nashville,
Tennessee, May 1985.

"The State of Nutrition Knowledge Among Physicians."
Paper presented to the California Area Health Education Center, Statewide Program Advisory Committee
Meeting and Annual Conference, Sacramento, May 1984.

"Feeding Patients Nutritional Advice: Tasting What We Dish Out."
Paper presented at University of California, Davis, Family Practice Residency Network Conference,
Yosemite, California, March 1984.

"The Barefoot Doctors of Mexico's Oil Boom."
Paper presented to the University of California, Davis, Family Practice Residency Network Conference,
March 1981.

"Delivery of Health Care in Craig, Alaska."
Paper presented to the University of Washington, Department of Family Practice, September 1978.

BRADLEY MICHAEL LEWIS

72 Hilltop Road
San Francisco, California 94117
(415) 222-XXXX

BACKGROUND SUMMARY

Extensive experience in sales, marketing, and finance in the mortgage industry. Series 7 and 63 Registered Representative.

Consistently satisfy customer needs and generate new business.

Expertise in increasing productivity by initiating and implementing automated marketing systems. Highly skilled in transforming complex tasks into manageable operations.

EDUCATION

M.B.A., concentration in Finance and Accounting, **HARVARD BUSINESS SCHOOL**, Cambridge, Massachusetts

B.S., concentration in Engineering and Mathematics, **YALE UNIVERSITY**, New Haven, Connecticut

EXPERIENCE

GOLDEN GATE MORTGAGE CORPORATION, San Francisco, California, 1988 - present

VICE PRESIDENT - PORTFOLIO SERVICES

Successfully created a start-up Servicing Evaluation and Brokerage Business unit. Developed low-cost, efficient, automated operation using PCs and mainframe computer providing the highest productivity in the industry. Generated over 80% of the fees during the first 3 years of operation.

Analyzed value of portfolios using a PC-based model and excellent technical skills. Developed nationwide network of senior management contacts to add to strong West Coast base. Served as Regional Vice President for Secondary Marketing.

PACIFIC MORTGAGE, INC., San Francisco, California, 1986 - 1988

SENIOR VICE PRESIDENT - SECONDARY MARKETING

Managed Secondary Mortgage Marketing for a start-up mortgage banking company that was capitalized with $2.5 million from over 30 private investors. Closed over $105 million in mortgages in the first year and a half. Negotiated $8 million forward whole loan commitment that earned approximately $225,000 in marketing gains and $160,000 in servicing sale.

Developed personal computer models to assist in all phases of secondary marketing. Acquired specific knowledge of secondary marketing operations relating to Freddie Mac, Fannie Mae, Ginnie Mae, and FHA/VA loan programs, and secured approval to sell mortgage loans to these investors.

Headed the Risk Management and Marketing Committees. Managed and supervised secondary marketing and shipping departments and related staff. Developed network of key contacts in mortgage and MBS industries.

WESTERN MORTGAGE INSURANCE, San Francisco, California, 1985 - 1986

ACCOUNT EXECUTIVE - SECONDARY MARKETING

Facilitated short- and long-term mortgage product financing for a network of corporate mortgage insurance customers. Advised customers about regulation changes, government mortgage purchase programs, and alternative methods of mortgage sales. Analyzed alternatives for mortgage financing and recommended the best source of financing to customers. Passed the Series 7 and Series 63 NASD exams to become a registered securities sales representative.

ATLAS MORTGAGE, Los Angeles, California, 1984 - 1985

VICE PRESIDENT - SECONDARY MARKETING

Assisted in decision making and execution of GNMA/FHLMC trades. Developed thrift institution customers for sale of mortgage whole loans and MBS's.

HLP MORTGAGE INSURANCE, Los Angeles, California, 1983 - 1984

ACCOUNT EXECUTIVE - SECONDARY MARKETING

Maintained primary line contact with corporate mortgage insurance customers to assist them in obtaining short- and long-term financing for mortgage products.

Ranked in the top 3 of marketing directors in volume sold, 1984. Ranked second out of 12 marketing directors in volume sold and generated over $1 million in fee income, 1983.

FNM AMERICA, New York, New York, 1977 - 1983

DIRECTOR OF CORPORATE SPECIAL PROJECTS

Reported directly to Chief Operating Officer for $40 billion financial institution that is primary developer of the secondary market for conventional mortgages. Provided recommendations on corporate organizational, financial, management, and marketing issues relating to the development and implementation of a corporate Mortgage Marketing Department. Mortgage portfolio doubled to over $40 billion and profits doubled to over $60 million in one year as a result of recommendations.

Corporate representative on Conference for Pension Fund Investments that was established to attract pension funds to invest in mortgages or MBS's.

DIRECTOR OF FINANCIAL PLANNING

Managed asset/liability mix for corporation. Directly accountable for developing financial strategy to fund over $19 billion in mortgage purchases over three-year period through sales of MBS's or debt. Created financial analyses and strategies models. Provided Chief Executive Officer with first regular monthly and annual financial plans.

ASSISTANT TREASURER

Developed and supervised the preparation of cash budgets, cash flow forecasts, cash management projects, and profit forecasts. Initiate executed, and controlled short term investment and borrowing strategy for portfolio of $200 million to $1 b

LEADERSHIP ACTIVITIES

President, Yale Class Foundation that has provided over $400,000 in college grants to over 70 children of deceased classmates; directly responsible for raising almost $500,000.

Past President of Toastmasters Club; received award as **Outstanding Club President** for 32-club division.

Past Executive Committee Member, Harvard Club of San Francisco.

JUANITA ALVAREZ-DIXON
32 Main Street, Tulsa, Oklahoma 74100
Work (918) 666-XXXX Home (918) 555-XXXX

CAREER SUMMARY

Over 25 years of progressively responsible positions with Tulsa Public Schools. Principal of a historic black elementary school for the past 17 years. Perpetuate historic nature of the school. Initiate creative alternatives to keep school a viable and integrated part of the community. Provide a setting establishing ownership between the community, parents, and teachers.

- Instrumental in developing alternative solution to avoid closing a historic black school. Totally designed and implemented a gifted center to merge with the community school, grades 3 - 6.
- Incorporated a learning disability center into the community school (L.D. Immersion Model). Developed and implemented an integration and immersion program with the community school and gifted center.
- Invited to present workshops for Oklahoma State Department of Education on special education issues and the successful L.D. Immersion Model.
- Established a special education parent support group providing a forum for parents to exchange concerns and to educate parents on their legal rights.

EXPERIENCE

TULSA PUBLIC SCHOOLS

PRINCIPAL, 1976 - present
Madeline Smith Elementary School, Tulsa, Oklahoma

ASSISTANT PRINCIPAL, 1974 - 1976
Sandy Lane Elementary School, Tulsa, Oklahoma

TEACHER/TEAM LEADER, 1969 - 1974
Green Hills Elementary School, Tulsa, Oklahoma

EXPERIENCE HIGHLIGHTS

- Frequent speaker, "How to Network Community Involvement in the School System," at local civic association meetings.
- Advisory Board, Guest Speaker, and Workshop Coordinator, "Successful Techniques for Working with Parents" and "Proactive Strategies For Responsible Behaviors," at University of Tulsa, School of Education.
- Coordinator of Jefferson Pyramid (all local schools feeding into Jefferson High School).
- Member, Tulsa Minority Achievement Committee.
- Taught graduate courses in "School Community Relations" and "Techniques for Behavior Change," Oklahoma State University, Oklahoma City, Oklahoma and Francis College (Tulsa Public Schools, Staff Development Program).
- Served on implementation team, Tulsa Public Schools, introducing team teaching and learning centers.

EDUCATION

Post-Master's work, UNIVERSITY OF TULSA, Tulsa, Oklahoma

M.S. in Administration and Supervision, 1972, OKLAHOMA STATE UNIVERSITY, Oklahoma City, Oklahoma

B.A. in Education, 1966, TEXAS SOUTHERN UNIVERSITY, Houston, Texas

AWARDS/HONORS

Appreciation awards for work training programs, **Outstanding Service to Tulsa Juvenile and Domestic Court**, 1981 - present

Tulsa Tribune, **Commendation for Educational Leadership**, 1986, 1987, 1989, 1992

PTA Honor, renovated courtyard renamed and dedicated, **"The Juanita Alvarez-Dixon Courtyard,"** 1991

Nominee, **National PTA Phoebe Apperson Hearst Outstanding Education Award**, 1986

Superboss Award, outstanding human relations and recognition of professional status of secretaries and office personnel, Tulsa Association of Office Personnel, 1980

PUBLICATIONS

"Integration and Immersion - A School with Experience," *Oklahoma Journal of Education,* Fall 1993.

"Human Relations - A Matter for Principals," *Human Relations News Letter Vol.1,* Tulsa Public Schools, June 1989.

"HARMONY - Implementing a Gifted Center in a Community School," *Tulsa Journal of Education,* May 1983.

"What Teachers Should Expect From Their Administrators," *Tulsa Journal of Education,* April 1977.

"Snips and Snails and Ol Wives' Tales," (a study of sexism in the elementary school), *Tulsa Journal of Education,* October 1976.

"Turning on to Team Teaching," *Tulsa Journal of Education,* October 1974.

"In the Math Lab," *Teacher,* May-June 1974.

"Around the World in 60 Minutes," *Teacher,* October 1973.

OLIVER WILSON LINTON
9 Freeport Road
Sacramento, California 95820

Work (916) 888-XXXX
Home (916) 777-XXXX

EXPERIENCE

STATE OF CALIFORNIA, Sacramento, California
PRINTING DIRECTOR, 1986 - present

Direct in-plant printing facility for state government and administer printing procurement budget of $1.8 million. Direct supplies and maintenance accounts of approximately $500,000. Manage 40 production and supervisory employees; hire, appraise performance, counsel, promote, and take corrective action.

. Purchased and installed state-of-the-art pre-press, press, and bindery equipment in production areas. Implemented environmental and safety methods and procedures ensuring employee safety and comfort.

. Enhanced plant security procedures increasing document accountability. Improved product work flow and employee productivity by reorganizing and reworking production operations.

. Developed five-year plan for plant equipment, requirements, and staffing. Participated in developing specifications for a computerized production control system. Established production time standards for in-house scheduling and employee productivity analysis.

. Revised and rewrote all employee position descriptions and adjusted wage rates to bring salaries in line with other comparable state printing facilities.

PRINTING SPECIALIST, 1983 - 1985

Supported mission and goals in Quality Assurance Division. Met requirements and schedules by developing methods and procedures for monitoring in-house critical production jobs.

. Co-developed and implemented the first large-scale, comprehensive waste/spoilage system for the state production facilities and established a master plan of intended methodology, goals, and objectives. Purchased and installed waste measuring equipment in various production areas.

. Developed data collection and reporting methods utilizing computerized management information resources. Trained production employees in efficient equipment operation and data collection. Briefed upper-level managers on project concept and status.

PRINTING SPECIALIST, 1980 - 1983

Provided technical support to internal audit team; explored and assessed in-house waste, fraud, and abuse. Developed a comprehensive plan for auditing a printing plant; reviewed job estimating and planning procedures, inventory control, waste/spoilage controls, financial and budget data, work flow, and employee and equipment productivity.

PRINTING OFFICER, 1978 - 1980

Directed all field plant production operations and supervised a staff of 7 line supervisors and 100 production employees. Assigned work and ensured production schedules were met. Purchased and installed new production equipment throughout plant. Developed studies and statistical data to pinpoint problem areas of high waste and low equipment and employee productivity.

CITY OF LOS ANGELES, Los Angeles, California
ASSISTANT PRINTING MANAGER, 1976 - 1978

Purchased production equipment for the city printing facility. Developed equipment specifications, acceptance criteria, and installation plans. Performed analysis on existing plant methods and procedures, improving employee and equipment productivity and work flow. Performed cost analysis on printing methods to determine machine and product break-even points. Developed and implemented production time standards from historical and time-motion data.

INDUSTRIAL TECHNICIAN, 1974 - 1976

Planned and implemented a variety of production requirements utilizing sheet-fed and web printing equipment. Planned production cycle from beginning to end using imposition guides, working dummies, equipment specifications, and plant materials.

EDUCATION

Anticipate **Master of Science in Technology Management**, UNIVERSITY OF CALIFORNIA AT DAVIS, Davis, California, Summer 1994

Bachelor of Science in Printing Management, CALIFORNIA POLYTECHNIC STATE UNIVERSITY, San Luis Obispo, California, 1974

MAUREEN CLANCY

88 Good Luck Lane
Cambridge, Massachusetts 02138
Work (617) 888-XXXX Home (617) 889-XXXX

BACKGROUND SUMMARY

Extensive progressive experience in computer programming, all phases of testing, systems analysis, and training using Total Quality Management (TQM). Technical expertise and highly effective interpersonal skills.

EXPERIENCE

MASSACHUSETTS BELL, Boston, Massachusetts

Process and Quality Assurance Manager/Trainer, Software Defined Network (SDN) Provisioning Data Center (PDC), 1990 - present

Utilize billing expertise to develop billing usage reports, enabling the PDC to confirm presubscription to SDN in the Local Exchange Companies (LECs).

- Facilitate quality improvement communication and problem solving among seven functional groups.

- Develop and utilize statistical process controls to support PDC process.

- Identify training requirements of Center (100 - 120 people) and provide or coordinate training for all 7 functional groups. Originate local training packages and job aids, present these courses, and support multi-manager, multi-functional groups within the PDC.

- Act as technical single point of contact for center, interfacing with Bell Labs developers. Serve as technical support subject matter expert.

- Project manage new service introductions through beta tests and trials.

- Computer environment: IBM mainframe, UNIX, Informix-SQL, IBM PC, MS-DOS, Microsoft Word, WordPerfect, Professional Write, SQC Troubleshooter.

Project Team Leader/Systems Analyst, Software Defined Network (SDN), 1985 - 1989

Co-led initial development, implementation, and consequent enhancements of new billing system for Software Defined Network (SDN).

- Extensively created test plans and executed unit, system, intersystem, and user acceptance tests.

- Developed data dictionaries and process flow charts using Excelerator.

- Interfaced with product marketing, product management, engineering organizations, sales account teams, and account inquiry centers. Provided optimal customer care and resolved customer concerns.

- Designed bill detail tapes for customers. Assisted in producing billing brochure for SDN account teams and customers. Created sample tapes, sample bills, and job aids for customers.

- Contributed as a member of a Massachusetts Bell corporate-wide task force to identify issues and recommend solutions on SDN service.

- Invited to SDN Users Association Conference, San Francisco, California, June 1989. Made billing presentations to customers and sales account teams.

- Computer environment: IBM mainframe, IMS, TOTAL, VSAM, COBOL, TSO/ISPF, JCL, IBM PC, MS-DOS, Excelerator.

Project Team Leader, Shared EPSCS Network (SEN), 1983 - 1985
Programmer/System Test Coordinator, Basic Packet Switching System (BPSS), 1983
Programmer, Customer Records Information System (CRIS), 1982 - 1983
Programmer/Project Team Leader, Management Order Control (MOC), 1980 - 1983
Programmer, Private Line Billing System, 1979 - 1980

Participated in teams developing and implementing new billing systems.

- Analyzed, designed, coded, tested, and implemented batch and online systems.

- Extensively created test plans and executed unit, system, intersystem, and user acceptance tests.

- Set quality standards for walkthroughs and system tests.

- Handled on-call production and maintenance problems.

- Computer environment: IBM mainframe, IMS, TOTAL, INTERCOMM, VSAM, COBOL, TSO/ISPF, JCL.

EDUCATION

Bachelor of Arts, Major: French, Minor: Mathematics, 1970
BOSTON COLLEGE, Chestnut Hill, Massachusetts

ANNE MARIE CICONI
8 Liberty Bell Lane
Philadelphia, Pennsylvania 19100
Work (215) 222-XXXX Home (215) 333-XXXX

CAREER SUMMARY

Experienced English professor, committed to developing programs and enriching college curriculum.

EDUCATION

Ph.D.,Bryn Mawr College, Bryn Mawr, Pennsylvania, 1977
M.A., Phi Kappa Phi, University of Pennsylvania, Philadelphia, Pennsylvania, 1972
B.A., cum laude, Beaver College, Glenside, Pennsylvania, 1959

CONTINUED EDUCATION

Pennsylvania Teaching Certification, (A) 1978
   Additional Course Work - Selected Topics:
   Morphology and Syntax, Beaver College, Glenside, Pennsylvania
   Improving Reading on the College Level, Bryn Mawr College, Bryn Mawr, Pennsylvania

FIELDS OF SPECIALIZATION

Primary Field: 18th Century British Literature
Secondary Fields: 19th Century British Literature; Composition
M.A. Thesis: The Novels of Charles Williams as Theological Mysteries
Ph.D.: Women's Published Autobiographies in the 18th Century

COURSES TAUGHT

American Literature, British Literature, Freshman English, Women in Literature, Study Skills, Composition, Introduction to Literature, Advanced Writing, Introduction to the Novel

EMPLOYMENT

TEMPLE UNIVERSITY, Philadelphia, Pennsylvania, 1986 - present
   Professor of English, 1986 - present

BRYN MAWR COLLEGE, Bryn Mawr, Pennsylvania, 1977 - 1986
   Dean of Students, Associate Professor of English, 1981 - 1986
   Chair, Associate Professor of English, 1979 - 1981
   Assistant Professor of English, 1977 - 1979

UNIVERSITY OF PENNSYLVANIA, Philadelphia, Pennsylvania, 1975 - 1977
Instructor, Department of English

OHIO WESLEYAN UNIVERSITY, Delaware, Ohio, 1973 - 1975
Part-Time Instructor

UNIVERSITY OF PENNSYLVANIA, Philadelphia, Pennsylvania, 1970 - 1972
Teaching Assistant

STARK TECHNICAL COLLEGE, Canton, Ohio, 1967 - 1968
Part-Time Instructor in Remedial Education

BEAVER COLLEGE, Glenside, Pennsylvania, 1959 - 1960
Director of Student Programs

PROFESSIONAL DEVELOPMENT

Liberty Conference, **The Psychology of Women in Literature**, Philadelphia, Pennsylvania, Fall 1992

Counseling Institute, Trinity College, Washington, D.C., 1990

Evaluator Training Workshop, New York University, New York, New York, Summer 1989

College Leadership Summer Workshop, University of Illinois, Urbana, Illinois, 1988

Conference on Women: An Agenda for the Future, Cornell University, Ithaca, New York, May 1985

Educational Leadership in Colleges Conference, Curriculum Development, Sarah Lawrence College, Bronxville, New York, 1983

Conference on Balancing the Curriculum, Radcliffe College, Cambridge, Massachusetts, 1983

Conference on Equity and Excellence, Women's Studies and the Humanities, New York University, New York, New York, 1983

Lives and Times: A Seminar on Biography, College of Notre Dame, Baltimore, Maryland, Summer 1980

AMELIA CARTER-SAWYER
8 Wildwood Way
New Haven, Connecticut 06520
(203) 889-XXXX

CAREER SUMMARY

Experienced attorney with a background in the private and public sectors. Expertise with telecommunications, public utilities, administrative, and environmental law issues.

EXPERIENCE

Yale University School of Law, New Haven, Connecticut
ADJUNCT PROFESSOR, 1992 - present

Teach course in "Legal Research, Writing, and Analysis."

Tutors Unlimited, New Haven, Connecticut
TUTOR, 1989 - present

Tutor students in LSAT preparation, English composition and grammar, and economics.

Miller, Samuelson & Associates, Washington, D.C.
ASSOCIATE, 1985 - 1988

Secured Intelecom as client, providing basis of firm's Federal Communication Commission practice. Project manager for successful filing of over 300 cellular applications. Assisted, advised, and wrote guidelines for telecom and start-up company clients on a variety of business and regulatory matters. Handled wide range of contract negotiations.

Wrote article, "Assessing Abandoned Mining Land Reclamation Fees On Coal," published in *West Virginia Law Review*, Spring 1986.

Intelecom Incorporated, Washington, D.C.
ASSISTANT GENERAL COUNSEL, 1983 - 1985

Established state regulatory program for the development stage of company engaged in cellular radio telephone and paging services. Filed and prosecuted applications with state utility commissions for authority to operate, complied with state "doing business" requirements, hired and managed local counsel. Accomplished objective of bringing all Federal regulatory legal work in-house. Advised and represented clients in business matters related to partnerships and commencement of cellular service.

U.S. Environmental Protection Agency, Washington, D.C.
ENFORCEMENT ATTORNEY, Office of Enforcement Counsel, 1981 - 1983

Prepared and assisted in litigation of stationary source Clean Air Act cases. Managed complex discovery in major District Court case, thereby ending two-year stalemate. Brought several stale cases either to settlement or to resolution in District Court.

ATTORNEY/ADVISOR, Office of Air, Noise, and Radiation, 1980 - 1981

Analyzed legal, technical, and economic merits of automobile manufacturers' applications for waivers of air pollution standards, and wrote decisions having immediate impact on private diesel automobile manufacturers. Coordinated intra-agency waiver reviews, evaluated California motor vehicle regulations, and assisted in long-range regulatory planning.

EDUCATION

YALE UNIVERSITY SCHOOL OF LAW, New Haven, Connecticut
Juris Doctor, cum laude, 1980

Staff Member, *Journal of International Law and Economics*; Recipient, Trustees' Scholarship; Moot Court; Community Legal Clinic

UNIVERSITY OF CONNECTICUT, Storrs, Connecticut
Bachelor of Arts, Economics, magna cum laude, 1977

Honors Program; Freshman Women's Honor Society

BAR MEMBERSHIPS

Connecticut, District of Columbia

SUZANNE CHAN

3118 Bay Street

Oakland, California 94608

Work (510) 777-XXXX Home (510) 666-XXXX

SUMMARY OF QUALIFICATIONS

Extensive experience as an imaginative and creative public relations professional. Work effectively under pressure, undertaking multiple projects simultaneously and shifting priorities with ease.

- Diplomatic interpersonal skills; excellent writer and speaker.

EXPERIENCE

PUBLIC RELATIONS DIRECTOR

ASSOCIATION OF ANTI-HUNGER, San Francisco, California, 1991 - present

Design and direct media campaigns on hunger issues for anti-hunger advocacy organization. Develop media strategies, events, and materials, and manage press lists and mailings. Oversee a network of 1,300 national media activists.

- Staged media event "Hunger Hurts." Received national press coverage and 90-second spot on national news.
- Designed and placed advertisement in ten national newspapers depicting national plight of the hungry.

PUBLIC RELATIONS DIRECTOR

NATIONAL HISTORICAL WOMEN, Washington, D.C., 1989 - 1991

Planned, managed, and coordinated news releases, printed materials, and advertising for national service organization with over 175,000 members.

- Promoted positive community and media relations by exploring new public image activities.
- Established effective relationships with media and state public relations coordinators.
- Collaborated with Historical Foundation in developing and sponsoring activities and programs, culminating in the establishment of the Historical Monument Park in 1993.
- Conceived and placed 4-page advertisement in 4 national newspapers and 3 national magazines portraying women's role in American history.

PUBLIC RELATIONS ASSISTANT

MONTGOMERY COUNTY PARK AUTHORITY, Rockville, Maryland, 1985 - 1989

Promoted parks and recreation through effective media relations and publicity campaigns. Designed and produced recreation brochure of calendar of special events and class offerings at recreation sites.

- Improved community relations; conducted surveys and held town meetings to identify community needs and concerns. Implemented and publicized family passes and discount vouchers.

EDUCATION

Bachelor of Arts in English, The American University, Washington, D.C., 1985

WAYNE WRIGHT
88 Second Avenue, New York, New York 10002
(212) 888-XXXX

QUALIFICATIONS SUMMARY

Sixteen years experience in writing, editing, and hands-on publication management.

- Effectively develop and coordinate projects from budgeting, copy editing, and generating stories to project oversight, design, and layout.
- Work closely with writers to successfully improve copy and translate complex ideas into understandable prose.

WORK HISTORY

Print Media

- Associate Editor of newsletter, *Inside the Market*, with circulation of 20,000, and stock report, *Stocks: Hot Picks*, Market Publishers Inc. 1991 - present.
- Associate Editor of newsletter, *Business Home Base*, with circulation of 12,000, New Business Publications. 1989 - 1991.
- Founding Editor and Partner of *Memphis Business Report*, a monthly tabloid with circulation of 15,000. Directed editorial and production for more than 1,500 pages a year. Handled concurrent responsibilities of Editor-in-Chief, Managing Editor, Copy Editor, and Production Manager. Supervised a staff of 7. 1982 - 1989.
- *Memphis Business Report* received 16 national awards for editorial and graphic excellence during leadership tenure.
- Received two national writing awards, *Memphis Business Report*.
- City Editor and Reporter, *Memphis Enterprise*, a community weekly with circulation of 40,000. 1980 - 1982.
- Reporter, *City City*, alternative weekly in Memphis with circulation of 10,000. 1979.

Radio and Television

- Numerous appearances on Tennessee Public Broadcasting. 1988 - 1989.
- Host, "Business Edition," cable public access channel, 30-minute live call-in program. 1987.
- Monthly guest, "Economy Issues," WDDS-AM radio, 15-minute talk show. 1987 - 1989.
- Commentator, "Business Issues," WSSX-FM, twice-weekly 90-second business commentary, morning and evening drive time. 1985 - 1986.
- Frequent guest on TV talk shows concerning the economy. 1986 - 1989.

RELEVANT SKILLS

Public Speaking

- Frequent speaker to civic groups in Memphis area on economic outlook and business trends.
- Recurrent guest lecturer, Memphis University journalism classes, on business and feature writing.

Teaching

- Conducted seminar on "Trends in Business Writing" at Association of Southern Newspaper Publishers Association conference in Memphis, Tennessee, January 1989.
- Taught "Magazine Editing and Writing," short courses, and conference programs at University of Tennessee, Memphis, Tennessee.
- Taught "Principles of Magazine Editing" at Tennessee State University, Nashville, Tennessee.

EDUCATION

Bachelor of Arts, Journalism, 1979
TENNESSEE STATE UNIVERSITY, Nashville, Tennessee

PROFESSIONAL AFFILIATIONS

Memphis Press Club

RABBI RACHEL LEVINE

6788 Dupont Circle
Washington, D.C. 20008
Work (202) 333-XXXX Home (2021) 334-XXXX

A dynamic leader with a creative approach in developing programs encouraging spiritual growth and integrating Judaism into our lives. Special interest and expertise in working with families with young children, senior adults, and interfaith couples. Extensive lecturing to Jewish organizations and other groups in metropolitan Washington D.C. area.

- Innovative outreach and life-cycle ceremonies including weddings and baby-namings.
- Frequently appear on local television, radio programs, and in local press.

PROFESSIONAL EXPERIENCE

Associate Rabbi, 1986 - present
TEMPLE B'NEI MITZVAH, Washington, D.C.

Professorial Lecturer, 1982 - 1990
THE AMERICAN UNIVERSITY, Washington, D.C.
Jewish Studies Program/Department of Religion and Philosophy
"Judaism and Christianity in Dialogue"

Rabbi/Director, 1980 - 1985
B'NAI B'RITH HILLEL FOUNDATION, THE AMERICAN UNIVERSITY, Washington, D.C.

Seminar Leader, 1982
WESLEY THEOLOGICAL SEMINARY, Washington, D.C.
"Ministering to the Academic Community: Interfaith Cooperation and Dialogue"

Lecturer, 1982
ELDER SEMINAR, AMERICAN JEWISH CONGRESS, Washington, D.C.
"History of Jewish-Christian Relations"

COMMUNAL ACTIVITIES

JEWISH COMMUNITY CENTER OF GREATER WASHINGTON
Advisory Board, Interfaith Outreach Committee, 1992 - present

UNION OF AMERICAN HEBREW CONGREGATIONS
Interreligious Affairs Committee, Mid-Atlantic Region, 1989 - present
Advisory Board, Department of Interreligious Affairs, 1988 - present

MA'ALOT (School for Cantors and Jewish Communal professionals)
Vice President, 1990 - present

CHEVY CHASE CLERGY ASSOCIATION
Vice President, 1989 - 1990

FORMER MEMBER
BOARD OF JEWISH EDUCATION OF GREATER WASHINGTON: Executive Council
CENTRAL CONFERENCE OF AMERICAN RABBIS: Committee on Justice and Peace
WOMEN'S RABBINIC NETWORK: Co-ordinator

EDUCATION

RABBINIC

HEBREW UNION COLLEGE-JEWISH INSTITUTE OF RELIGION, New York, New York
Rabbinic Ordination, June 1980

Honors

The Alan N. Weisman Memorial Prize in Homiletics to a Senior Student
The Stephen S. Wise Prize for General Excellence
The Rabbi Hugo Hahn Memorial Prize for a Student Excelling in the Study of History
The Molly and Benjamin Borowitz Memorial Award in Jewish Religious Thought
The Rabbi Jerome R. Malino Annual Freshman Award

GRADUATE

HEBREW UNION COLLEGE, JEWISH INSTITUTE OF RELIGION, New York, New York
Master of Arts in Hebrew Literature, December 1978

THE CATHOLIC UNIVERSITY OF AMERICA, SCHOOL OF RELIGIOUS STUDIES, Washington, D.C.
Graduate courses (6 credits), 1980 - 1981

THE DROPSIE UNIVERSITY, Philadelphia, Pennsylvania
Graduate Fellow in Comparative Religion, 1973 - 1974
Advanced ulpan and seminar: The Haim Greenberg Institute in Jerusalem, Summer 1973

UNDERGRADUATE

YALE UNIVERSITY, New Haven, Connecticut
Bachelor of Arts, cum laude, 1973
Major: Religious Studies
Junior Year Abroad: The Hebrew University in Jerusalem, 1971 - 1972

PUBLICATIONS

Sermons

The American Rabbi
"The Missing 'Hineini': Rosh Hashanah," 1992
"Our Love of Nature: Tu B'Shvat," December 1991
"Daughters of Israel Speak Up: Parshat Pinchas," December 1990
"Secrets and Discoveries: Lilith - Parshat Bereshit," April 1989
"Is the Norm Enough?" June 1988
"Self Acceptance," October 1987
"The Quiet Sabbath," April 1987
"Gardens of Memory," December 1984

Articles

UME Connexion, Fall 1982
NICM Journal, Spring and Summer 1983
"Promoting Interfaith Dialogue"

PAUL T. HUGHES

5443 Palomino Road

Houston, Texas 77027

Work (713)999-XXXX Home (713) 888-XXXX

CAREER SUMMARY

Senior Executive with management background in design, construction, and operations with organizational responsibility of up to 250 people.

Successfully create new business opportunities and improve/expand existing operations. Deliver large, complex commercial programs on time and within budget.

EXPERIENCE

SOUTHERN DEVELOPMENT CORPORATION, Houston, Texas

SENIOR VICE PRESIDENT - DEVELOPMENT SERVICES GROUP, 1989 - present

Manage all development services for super regional-size projects including site planning, engineering, design, construction, and tenant administration. Contribute expertise and recommendations from land acquisition and predevelopment through design, construction, and property management support.

Directed close-out operations at Harper Mills, Philadelphia; construction and grand opening of Colton Mills, Detroit; design and construction of Sunset Mills, Phoenix; planning/preliminary design of Ash Mills, Chicago.

LIBERTY CITY COMMERCIAL CONSTRUCTION CO., INC. (LCCCI), Philadelphia, Pennsylvania

PRESIDENT, 1988 - 1989

Promoted to President/CEO of a subsidiary construction organization of Liberty City Enterprises, one of the largest national real estate development firms with regional offices in Boston, New York, Los Angeles, and Tucson.

Executed all design, construction, and tenant administration related activities for commercial projects developed by Liberty City Enterprises. Annual 1988 - 1989 volumes of actual work in place were approximately $250 - $300 million.

EXECUTIVE VICE PRESIDENT, 1986 - 1988

Initially assigned one-half of all LCCCI projects under construction. Re-organized all internal project estimating, scheduling, cost accounting, and management reporting systems.

WORTHY'S, New York, New York

SENIOR VICE PRESIDENT - REAL ESTATE PLANNING DIVISION, 1981 - 1983

Directed Worthy's Real Estate Development program including store planning, store design, drafting, construction, visual merchandising, accounting, and administrative departments. Coordinated with the Real Estate Group of National Department Stores, Inc., in Atlanta.

Opened three new stores in Houston, Texas, Orlando, Florida, and Philadelphia, Pennsylvania. Coordinated major renovation of New York City store and all on-going store design and construction programs throughout Worthy's.

ALLIED CONSTRUCTION, INC., Los Angeles, California

PRESIDENT/CEO, 1981

Progressive promotions to President/CEO of one of the largest general contracting firms operating nationally and specializing in retail/office/hotel-type commercial construction. Directed all activities of company with concentration on sales, long-range planning, and client development.

SENIOR EXECUTIVE VICE PRESIDENT/CHIEF OPERATING OFFICER, 1980 - 1981

Managed the five major operating divisions: Retail Operations, Hotel/Office Operations, Discount Retail Operations, Administrative Services, and Financial/Accounting Services.

Planned and directed the on-time, within budget, high-quality production of all work and the financial planning; management information services; and legal, estimating, and human resources support required to achieve corporate goals. Annual construction volume approximately $150 million.

EXECUTIVE VICE PRESIDENT/OPERATING DIVISION, 1979 - 1980

Directed day-to-day construction activities of Allied's four operating divisions. Developed project contracts and executed all construction.

EMPIRE COMPANY, New York, New York

VICE PRESIDENT/DIRECTOR OF ENGINEERING AND CONSTRUCTION, 1974 - 1979
SENIOR PROJECT MANAGER, 1972 - 1974
PROJECT MANAGER, 1970 - 1972

Progressive promotions to positions of increased responsibility for a retail, office, and new community development firm known for pioneering many innovative and state-of-the-art techniques for new community developments, in addition to regional, specialty, festival, and urban multi-use type development projects.

Managed on-time, high-quality construction of all Empire's development projects in excess of $300 million. Placed approximately $200 million of actual construction on-line during an 18 month period, 1977 - 1978.

Provided support for all capital improvement and major maintenance programs with a combined annual budget of approximately $4 million.

EDUCATION

Pursued degree in engineering at New York University, New York, New York

GUEST LECTURED
    Wharton School, University of Pennsylvania, "Construction Management Process"
    ICSC University of Shopping Centers, "Project Feasibility"
    University of Chicago Business School, "Shopping Center Development"

PROFESSIONAL DEVELOPMENT
    J. L. Kellogg Graduate School of Management, Northwestern University, "Executive Development Program"
    Fairfield University, "Aetna Life & Casualty's Advanced Management Course"
    Numerous design, construction, project management, and development related seminars

BRENDA BRADLEY

8 NW Second Avenue, Delray Beach, Florida 33445
Work (407) 498-XXXX Home (407) 488-XXXX

BACKGROUND SUMMARY

Efficient and well-organized Office Assistant with excellent verbal communication skills. Handle busy phone lines professionally and pleasantly.

Enthusiastic, people person with a desire to work diligently and grow with an organization.

SKILLS

Proficient with IBM PC and WordPerfect; Typing 45 wpm.
Familiar with Rolm and multi-line telephone systems.

EXPERIENCE

Receptionist
BOCA SUITES, Boca Raton, Florida, 1992 - present

Maintain a console of 20 phone lines for multi-firm suite. Greet and sign in visitors, perform general office duties; type letters and reports, arrange courier service, and assist other departments as needed.

Receptionist
DELRAY PEDIATRICS, Delray Beach, Florida, 1990 - 1992

Created and maintained files for new and established patients in a busy pediatric practice. Handled phones and scheduled appointments. Contacted and reminded patients of appointments. Typed correspondence to insurance companies and other physicians.

Office Assistant
PJK CONSTRUCTION COMPANY, Boca Raton, Florida, 1988 - 1990

Performed office duties for construction company. Received, screened, and routed calls, and maintained files. Distributed incoming mail and processed outgoing mail.

EDUCATION

Attend evening classes at **Palm Beach Community College**, Lake Worth, Florida
Completed adult education classes in **WordPerfect** and **Business English**

REBECCA MCKEE
654 Maple Avenue
Corning, New York 14831
(607) 888-XXXX

QUALIFICATIONS SUMMARY: Progressive experience and expertise in administrative and financial operations.

EXPERIENCE

CORNING SCHOOL DISTRICT, Corning, New York

Registrar/Financial Secretary, Corning High School, 1989 - present

Manage all school records, transcripts, diplomas, and senior graduation. Administer site-based management funds, budgets, and all school activity funds accounting for $500,000 in receipts and disbursements during school year.

Perform activity fund records management; record and reconcile all accounts payables, receivables, and transfers. Process and monitor all school fund raising activities, purchase orders, and related reports. Coordinate purchases with staff, district administration, and vendors. Received exceptional ratings on audits performed on school's books of accounts.

Attendance Clerk, Cobb Intermediate School, 1987 - 1989

Handled student enrollment and withdrawal. Prepared and processed daily attendance reports and contacted parents to verify validity of students' absences. Input all student information into district's computerized information management system (CIMS). Coordinated order and receipt of material shipments with data processing department.

Records Clerk, District Records and Attendance Administration, 1987

Compiled and processed cumulative grade reports for entire school district. Processed records verifications, transcripts, and requests for cumulative student records. Assisted in processing enrollments and withdrawals. Reviewed and corrected school computer input sheets prior to processing. Updated student records with district's CIMS. Answered telephones and processed mail.

RELATED EXPERIENCE

Held a variety of administrative positions 1975 - 1982. Performed general office and accounting duties including typing, bookkeeping, billing accounts, processing orders, maintaining records, and reconciling and balancing accounts.

SKILLS

Typing, 55 wpm; proficient with computer systems and WordPerfect.

EDUCATION

Attended classes at Corning Community College, Corning, New York, 1976 - 1977

EDUARDO GONZALEZ
14 Rose Hill Drive
San Francisco, California 94116
(415) 223-XXXX

Successful manager with extensive experience in all facets of restaurant operations.

EXPERIENCE

GENERAL MANAGER
Cafe Normandy, San Francisco, California, 1992 - present

Manage a mid-size French restaurant serving breakfast, lunch, and dinner. Supervise a staff of 25: recruit, interview, hire, train, review performance, counsel, and terminate employment. Compose and place advertising and create daily specials. Order liquors and wines.

MANAGER
Bay Street Restaurant and Bay Inn, Monterey, California, 1988 - 1991

Managed five-star and casual restaurants with a total seating capacity of 1,045. Supervised a staff of 100: recruited, interviewed, hired, reviewed performance, counseled, and terminated employment. Organized and conducted daily in-house training sessions. Ordered wines and liquors.

Coordinated banquets for 50 - 700 people. Selected and priced food, organized seating arrangements, scheduled and assigned staff, and ensured customer satisfaction.

MANAGEMENT TRAINEE
La Cantina, Santa Cruz, California, 1987 - 1988

Promoted to management trainee. Developed skills in day-to-day operations including staff scheduling, crew training, inventory control, cash handling, and customer service.

EDUCATION

Certified Food Service Manager, 1990
Marin County Government, Department of Health

Associate in Applied Science, major in Food Service, 1986
Santa Rosa Junior College, Santa Rosa, California

FRANK BENNETT

6 Silent Oak Street, Dayton, Ohio 45463
Work (513) 999-XXXX Home (513) 888-XXXX

| CORPORATE SECURITY AND SAFETY SPECIALIST |

EXPERIENCE

ABC COMPANY, Dayton, Ohio, 1986 - present

SENIOR SAFETY AND SECURITY SPECIALIST

Administer a safety awareness and security program for computer corporation with Department of Defense (DOD) contracts. Initiate and implement safety programs and guidelines. Evaluate and improve physical security, industrial security, and loss prevention programs.

As Control Center Operator, supervise access procedures, security tours, hazardous/sensitive areas, emergency response, and DOD procedures.

SMITH & ASSOCIATES, Dayton, Ohio, 1982 - 1986

SECURITY MANAGER

Supervised and scheduled 28 security officers for organization providing security for corporations, hospitals, department stores, and banks. Managed departmental budget of $1.35 million. Developed and implemented training programs, and revised and updated procedural manuals. Supervised an administrative support staff of 20.

OHIO DEPARTMENT OF CORRECTIONS, 1979 - 1982

EXECUTIVE OFFICER

Managed parole board office operation. Supervised and trained an office support staff of 16. Prepared agency budget.

Acted as liaison between Governor's office, correctional institutions, and federal, state, and local law enforcement agencies. Counseled juveniles delinquents, developed guidance objectives, and coordinated privileges and final release proceedings.

ILLINOIS DEPARTMENT OF CORRECTIONS, 1976 - 1979

CORRECTIONAL OFFICER/COUNSELOR

Supervised 175 male inmates in a minimum security prison with emphasis on custody, control, and rehabilitation.

EDUCATION

Bachelor of Science, Administration of Justice, 1976
UNIVERSITY OF ILLINOIS AT CHICAGO, Chicago, Illinois

Professional Development
Numerous courses in Industrial Security

MICHAELA FRENCH

4667 Riverside Drive
New Orleans, Louisiana 70110
(504) 221-XXXX

BACKGROUND SUMMARY

Highly motivated, self-starter seeking a sales position with unlimited growth opportunities. Excellent communication and interpersonal skills and strong desire to build a career in the television industry.

EDUCATION

Bachelor of Arts in Economics, 1993
TULANE UNIVERSITY, New Orleans, Louisiana

EXPERIENCE

SOUTHERN PROMOTIONS, New Orleans, Louisiana
Owner of Marketing Company, 1991 - present

Established a successful marketing promotions business. Sell advertisement services to cleaners and independently owned automotive repair facilities, such as Goodyear. Write advertising copy, contract printing services, and conduct door-to-door sales. Handle all administrative operations.

WALT DISNEY WORLD CO., Lake Buena Vista, Florida
Tour Guide for the Disney-MGM Studio Backlot, August 1992 - January 1993

Nationally selected from over 12,000 applicants to participate in the living, working, and learning experience of the Walt Disney World College Program.

Conducted tours of the Disney-MGM Studio Backlot to more than 4,000 guests a week. Interacted with people from all over the world and provided quality guest service.

Attended 10 business seminars (30 hours) designed to teach the management philosophies of the Walt Disney Co. and lived with international students in a multicultural environment.

Selected among 500 Disney employees to represent Disney in a national commercial, shown during 1993 on prime time television.

WADA 104.7, New Orleans, Louisiana
Promotion Assistant, June 1988 - January 1991

Distributed promotional prizes at concerts and other major events for radio station. Set up equipment for live broadcasts. Drove the WADA 21-foot radio trailer.

WILLING TO RELOCATE

STEPHEN A. VICKERS

99 Nash Drive
Detroit, Michigan 48214
Work (313) 444-XXXX Home (313) 555-XXXX

Senior Sales Executive with management background in sales, marketing, finance, and operations with organizational responsibility of up to 70 people.

EXPERIENCE

MANAGER OF FEDERAL OPERATIONS
NATIONAL TECHNOLOGY, Detroit, Michigan, 1992 - present

♦ Manage all national federal accounts for a leading industrial parts corporation. Handle all GSA schedule negotiations. Administer an expense budget of $1 million.

♦ Initiated a successful marketing strategy. Increased sales from a flat $1.7 million to $4.2 million in first year.

♦ Recruited and developed an effective staff of 14.

REGIONAL DIRECTOR
E.P. SOFTWARE, INC., Washington, D.C., 1984 - 1991

♦ Established and managed federal and commercial sales operation for electronic publishing software operation. Built organization to $6 million in annual revenue. Recruited and managed a staff of 25 professionals.

♦ Generated business plans and worked with top corporate management to implement strategies. Developed and administered annual budget.

♦ Initiated and successfully negotiated a teaming arrangement with Automated Industries for the $350 million 600-S procurement to provide desktop publishing systems and software at all U.S. Army bases nationwide. Managed all U.S. federal marketing operations, with multi-million dollar contract awards from the intelligence community, defense, and civilian agencies.

DIRECTOR, FEDERAL MARKETING
FUTURE TECH, Washington, D.C., 1981 - 1984

♦ Increased revenue from $9 million to $43 million through sales and service of dedicated word processing systems for end-users in Department of Defense and civilian government agencies. Traveled to Europe to manage federal marketing on a worldwide basis. Negotiated annual GSA Schedule contracts and competitively awarded contracts.

♦ Directed a staff of 70 sales professionals, systems engineers, technical writers, and contract specialists for $200 million company.

♦ Played a leadership role in recruiting top producers in technical and marketing specialties to achieve ambitious targets for growth and profitability.

BRANCH MANAGER
TECHCON CORPORATION, Washington, D.C., 1976 - 1981

♦ Solid record of achievement and advancements as the manager of several high-profile branches and federal accounts for data processing corporation with $500 million in annual sales.

♦ Built a federal sales team that grew from 3 to 45 professionals. Developed and administered annual budget, controlled expenses, and maintained lowest expense-to-sale ratio in the company.

REGIONAL MANAGER
SCIENCE TECH INC., Washington, D.C., 1972 - 1976

♦ Developed and managed a network of manufacturers' representatives to market company's intelligent terminal and data entry products in the Southeastern region. Directed 4 field service engineers. Personal sales topped $2 million.

SALES EXECUTIVE
ABC MACHINES, Washington, D.C., 1970 - 1972

♦ Marketed mini computers for southeastern region of Advanced Systems Division. Closed the largest system configuration nationwide.

SALES EXECUTIVE
DATA PRO, Detroit, Michigan, 1966 - 1970

♦ Successfully marketed data processing equipment to the commercial sector. Annual performance exceeded 175% of quota. Top year exceeded 200% of annual quota. Conducted all branch sales training during last 2 years.

EDUCATION

Bachelor of Arts in Economics, 1966
Michigan State University, East Lansing, Michigan

Professional Development
Graduate of DATA PRO sales and management development program

Completed numerous seminars and programs offered through industry associations and manufacturers

CYNTHIA CRANE
7001 Sandy Court, Apartment 3D
Denver, Colorado 80201
(303) 777-XXXX

Experienced Sales/Marketing Professional

CAREER SUMMARY

Consistent top sales performer. Expertise in building and maintaining effective customer relations.

EXPERIENCE

CANNON SALES AGENT, 1992 - present
American Business Corporation, Denver, Colorado

Successfully develop and implement marketing strategies for Lakewood sales territory for Cannon copiers and facsimile machines. Build and maintain client base and customer loyalty through high-quality service delivery.

Employ a broad range of sales closing techniques and knowledge of customer purchasing objectives to increase sales volume.

Promoted to sales manager within two months. Train sales agents in writing proposals, marketing and closing techniques, and territory management.

- **Consistently achieve over 100% of sales targets.**
- **Top Agent, Denver Suburban District, January, February, April 1993.**
- **Achieved 127% of plan; 1st Quarter, 1993.**

MATHEMATICS TEACHER/SUBSTITUTE, 1990 - 1991
The Brown Academy, Denver, Colorado

Prepared curriculum and taught math to elementary grades and 9th - 10th grades.

EDUCATION

BACHELOR OF SCIENCE, Economics, 1991
UNIVERSITY OF COLORADO, Boulder, Colorado

PROFESSIONAL DEVELOPMENT
Completed five-week Cannon Sales Training Program
Top of training class in product demonstration and knowledge

References Furnished Upon Request

R. PETER BIRCH

8 Shore Drive, Providence, Rhode Island 02907
Work (401) 888-XXXX Home (401) 777-XXXX

Over 30 years of progressive experience in sales, purchasing, and operations management.

EXPERIENCE

PROVIDENCE ELECTRIC SUPPLY COMPANY, Providence, Rhode Island, 1978 - present

Commercial Sales Manager, 1988 - present

Prepare bids and successfully negotiate contracts for commercial lighting projects from $5,000 - $300,000. Sole responsibility for profit and loss on each project. Effectively work with factories and resolve problems to meet contract completion dates and obligations. Mediate problems between commercial lighting factories and clients. Supervise and train personnel in manager's absence.

Created and implemented a tracking system to identify the bid status of any project. Increased efficiency of department by eliminating duplicate work.

Residential Sales Manager, 1978 - 1988

Managed four large-scale lighting showrooms. Supervised personnel, sales, and contract negotiations. Coordinated advertising and purchased lighting products. Reported status of profit and loss and inventory control directly to the president.

Initiated several sales promotions to eliminate overstocked inventory. Increased stock turnover from 2.5 to 4.5 turns with increased profit.

ABC ELECTRONICS AND CAMERA, INC., Providence, Rhode Island, 1959 - 1978

Vice-President and Operations Manager, 1970 - 1978

Managed all operations of retail electronics, appliance, and camera store. Planned and directed purchasing, budget control, personnel, accounts payable and accounts receivable, customer relations, and sales. Skillfully handled company troubleshooting and problem-solving.

Analyzed the growth potential of camera department and increased gross and net profit of department by 40% within a 4-month period.

Effectively developed advertising layout and copy for daily print. Innovative merchandising techniques and personnel training generated a 50% increase in sales over a 3-year period. Planned and organized a priority payment schedule enabling merchandise to flow on a regular basis.

Vice-President and Sales Manager, 1965 - 1970

Managed departmental operations in sales, finance, and merchandising. Handled purchasing, budget control, personnel, accounts payable and accounts receivable, customer relations, and sales. Coordinated advertising and resolved problems. Acquired 25% ownership in the company.

Effectively selected procurement process which saved 5% - 10% on department purchases. Created and implemented an inventory profit and unit control system which enhanced purchasing ability, employee incentives, and accomplishments.

Service Manager and Salesman, 1959 - 1965

EDUCATION

Atlantic Technical Institute of Rhode Island, Providence, Rhode Island
    Completed one-year Electronics Program, 1961

DANIEL VOLLMER
54 Tulip Lane, Boise, Idaho 83702
Work (208) 555-XXXX Home (208) 777-XXXX

CAREER OBJECTIVE

A sales management position with a progressive firm offering the opportunity for career advancement and professional growth.

EXPERIENCE

REGIONAL MANAGER
U.S. COMMUNICATIONS, INC., Boise, Idaho, 1991 - present

Supervise a staff of 28 marketing specialized telecommunications services. Manage profitability of sales and operations for the western region. Increased net business by 41% by developing sales strategy for the region and streamlining operations.

ACCOUNT MANAGER
NATIONAL TECHNOLOGY, Spokane, Washington, 1991 - present

Managed database of 300 computer reseller accounts for computer distributor. Assisted and made recommendations in evaluating and acquiring new products. Top Salesman for 7 months.

SALES MANAGER
COMPUTER COMP, Philadelphia, Pennsylvania, 1988 - 1989

Managed 11 sales people marketing micro-computer products from several manufacturers to government and commercial accounts, as well as individual clients. Trained Junior Account Representatives in product knowledge and sales skills and scheduled and organized manufacturer sales training. Expertise with IBM compatible micro-computers, laser printers, dot matrix printers, monitors, and related peripherals.

ACCOUNT EXECUTIVE
NEWTECH, INC., Atlanta, Georgia, 1986 - 1988

Distributed and sold C.Itoh/CIE printers and terminals to dealers in the eastern United States. Assessed, organized, and implemented multiple bids to GSA vendors. Promoted to Eastern Regional Accounts Manger.

ACCOUNT EXECUTIVE
RESORTS INC., Atlanta, Georgia, 1984 - 1986

Contacted clients directly for sales and investment opportunities in resort development. Created, organized, and performed presentations involving the financial and tax advantages of international resort development. Promoted to Assistant Public Relations Manager.

SALES/FINANCE MANAGER
LITTON CHRYSLER, Macon, Georgia, 1981 - 1984

Sold new and used automobiles. Developed clientele through referral program. Promoted to Finance Account Manager. Winner of Salesman of the Month Award five times.

EDUCATION

Georgia State University, Atlanta, Georgia
Bachelor of Science in Economics, 1981, President of Young Entrepreneurs of Georgia

No restrictions on travel or relocation

GEORGIA T. GODFREY

6 Commonwealth Avenue
Boston, Massachusetts 02210
Work (617) 888-XXXX Home (617) 666-XXXX

BACKGROUND SUMMARY

Progressive experience in the airline industry marketing computerized reservation systems, training staff, and satisfying customer needs.

EXPERIENCE

AIRCOR CORPORATION, Boston, Massachusetts, 1987 - present

Senior Account Manager, 1988 - present

Effectively market airline reservations computer system to clients, assuring program meets requirements prior to final presentation. Maximize client use through productive training. Ensure client satisfaction.

Conduct hands-on training programs on the use of computer system. Provide one-on-one and group instruction, and tailor the material and program to the needs of the individuals and organization.

Conducted administrative training to over 100 field consultants. Revised "Consultant Manual."

Service Consultant, 1987 - 1988

Managed a territory of 60 accounts. Motivated the subscriber base to utilize the computer reservations system with on-site training. Conducted a variety of on-site training and seminars. Strengthened the relationship to the subscriber base with continued follow-up.

ABC AIRLINES, Washington, D.C., 1978 - 1987

Supervisor, Training and Quality Control, 1986 - 1987

Managed the recurrent training program for over 200 employees. Supervised 3 departments: Training, Customer Relations, and the Agent Assistance Desk. Administered the Quality Control Program. Coordinated the initial reservations training program.

Supervisor, General Sales, 1981 - 1986

Supervised 30 reservations agents. Interviewed and selected employees; reviewed job performance and counseled employees. Conducted recurrent training.

Reservations Agent, 1978 - 1981

Developed management potential in the Lead Agent Program. Relief Agent on the Help Desk for the Aircor subscribers.

RELATED EXPERIENCES

Instructor, Montgomery Community College, Rockville, Maryland, 1984
Taught an airline reservations program.

Elementary Teacher, Virginia and New Jersey, 1972 - 1979
Taught 2nd through 8th grade developmental and remedial reading.

EDUCATION

MASTER OF ARTS IN EDUCATION, 1975
George Mason University, Fairfax, Virginia

BACHELOR OF ARTS IN SOCIOLOGY, 1971
Boston College, Boston, Massachusetts
Dean's List, 1969 - 1970

SKILLS

Knowledge of French

PROFESSIONAL ORGANIZATIONS

American Society for Training and Development

ANTHONY WEBSTER
65 Oriole Drive
Bloomington, Indiana 47405
Work (812) 666-XXXX Home (812) 888-XXXX

Experienced clinician with an expertise in marriage and family psychotherapy and spousal and child abuse. Highly skilled in cultivating effective relationships and linkages with other professionals.

WORK HISTORY

Licensed Clinical Social Worker
Private Practice, Bloomington, Indiana, 1991 - present

Provide mental health treatment to adults, adolescents, children, couples, and families, and outpatient psychotherapy to patients on medication as prescribed by psychiatrists and other physicians.

Clinical Instructor
University of Indiana, Bloomington Family Center, Bloomington, Indiana, 1979 - present

Faculty member for post-graduate training programs in Family and Systems Theory and Family Psychotherapy for mental health professionals.

Emergency Mental Health Therapist
Bloomington Department of Human Services, Bloomington, Indiana, 1990 - 1991

Provided crisis intervention and emergency mental health services to clients. Directly involved with the Bloomington Police Department, other county agencies, and local hospitals in providing emergency services to clients in life-threatening situations.

Contract Mental Health Therapist
U.S. Army Medical Department, Arlington, Virginia, 1987 - 1990

Involved with preventing, identifying, reporting, investigating, and treating spouse and child maltreatment for the U.S. Army Family Advocacy Program.

Co-ordinator, Adult Services, Outpatient Unit
National Center for Community Mental Health, Arlington, Virginia, 1986 - 1987

Provided mental health services to adult and elderly patients and supervised mental health therapists.

Director, Community Mental Health Service
Walter Reed Army Medical Center, Washington, D.C., 1980 - 1985

Administered the mental health and social service programs at Walter Reed Health Clinic. Managed the Family Advocacy Case Management Team that treated child, spouse, and adult maltreatment cases.

Assistant Director, Human Resources Directorate
Director, Equal Opportunity
Walter Reed Army Medical Center, Washington, D.C., 1979 - 1980

Supervised the Affirmative Action Programs. Served as a consultant to the Chief Executive Officer/MD regarding organizational effectiveness, equal opportunity education, training, and affirmative action.

Director of Social Work
U.S. Army Medical Department Activity, Fort Knox, Kentucky, 1977 - 1979

Managed hospital's medical/surgical and psychiatric program. Developed one of the first comprehensive programs for rape victims and their families.

Assistant Director, Social Work
Walter Reed Army Medical Center, Washington, D.C., 1974 - 1977

Designed, organized, and wrote a thorough plan that established a multidisciplinary team to assist patients in the transition from hospital to home. Actively supervised other MSW and para-professional personnel.

Director, Army Community Service
Military District of Washington, Fort Myer, Virginia, 1973 - 1974

Developed, coordinated, and maintained human services programs to improve the quality of life and well-being of the community.

Director of Social Work
U.S. Army Medical Department, Fort Sill, Oklahoma, 1971 - 1973

Implemented social work as a separate hospital department. Devised methods to educate medical staff, patients, and the community as to the role of social work in the hospital and the community.

U.S. Army Medical Department, 1962 - 1971

Served in a variety of administrative and supervisory capacities in medical administration

EDUCATION

Post-Graduate Training Program in Family and Systems Theory and Family Psychotherapy, 1973 - 1977
GEORGETOWN UNIVERSITY MEDICAL CENTER, DEPARTMENT OF PSYCHIATRY,
Washington, D.C.

Master of Social Work, 1970
THE CATHOLIC UNIVERSITY OF AMERICA, Washington, D.C.

Bachelor of Arts, 1960
THE CITADEL, Charleston, South Carolina

LICENSES

Licensed Clinical Social Worker, Commonwealth of Virginia, Indiana

Licensed Independent Clinical Social Worker, Washington, D.C., Indiana

PROFESSIONAL AFFILIATIONS

Clinical Instructor, University of Indiana Family Center, Bloomington, Indiana

Clinical Member, American Association for Marriage and Family Therapy

Academy of Certified Social Workers, National Association of Social Workers

References Furnished Upon Request

ARTHUR G. FLETCHER
76 Live Oak Road, College Park, Maryland 20740
(301) 666-XXXX (H)(202) 555-XXXX (W)

QUALIFICATIONS SUMMARY

Twenty-nine years of progressive experience in the areas of investigation, justice, probation, and parole.

EXPERIENCE

Department of Justice, Washington, D.C.

Special Agent, 1971 - present

Conduct comprehensive investigations of high-profile, high-impact employers suspected of violating the administrative, civil and/or criminal provisions of the employer sanctions laws of the United States, as provided in the Immigration and Nationality Act (INA).

Initiate cases from leads, tips, and observations that arouse suspicion. Plan and conduct criminal investigations of document and marriage fraud, and conspiracy to defraud and violate immigration laws and criminal statutes. Utilize a thorough knowledge of criminal and immigration law, Federal criminal procedure, investigative techniques, rules of evidence, judicial processes and precedents, and the rights of aliens and criminal suspects.

Use a variety of sophisticated investigative techniques to develop cases: surveillance, interrogations, undercover methods, records interviews, examinations, cultivation and use of informants, search and arrest warrants, and subpoenas.

Present cases to the appropriate Service official for initiation of administrative proceedings. Assist U.S. Attorney's office in preparation of cases for presentation to Federal grand juries for trial: obtain, mark, and inventory evidence; prepare requests for document analysis; ensure preparation of exhibits for trial; and arrange for testimony by expert witnesses.

Prepare complete and comprehensive oral and written reports of case assignments.

Maryland Department of Corrections, Baltimore, Maryland

Correctional Treatment Specialist,1968 - 1971

Supervised parolees convicted and imprisoned for a variety of violent and non-violent crimes. Devised rehabilitation program, counseled family members and others to assist in parolee's adjustment, and ensured suitable working conditions. Achieved rehabilitative goals by utilizing skills in social work techniques, previous experiences, and sound judgment.

Maintained contact with parolee; provided counsel on home, employment, vocational, and marital issues; developed release plans for residence in half-way houses. Handled parolees relocating from other states; conducted interviews and provided instructions; explained obligations, instructions, and procedures; registered with proper authorities.

Conducted special investigations for out-of-state police departments, parole boards, probation departments, correction, detention, and penal institutions, and to locate parole violators. Handled a variety of reporting requirements and recommendations.

Pre-Parole Officer, 1967 - 1968

Reviewed and evaluated inmate parole applications. Contacted and interviewed individuals. Presented pre-parole plan with evaluation and analysis to be used by parole board as a guide.

Maryland Department of Public Welfare, Baltimore, Maryland

Social Service Representative, 1967

Performed full range of essential and auxiliary services for a case load of 60 families.

Maryland Re-Development Land Agency, Baltimore, Maryland

Family Relocation Counselor, 1966 - 1967

Ensured that individuals and families displaced by urban renewal, code enforcement, and public works projects were provided full range of services and assistance in relocation, reimbursements, and resources.

American National Red Cross, Philadelphia, Pennsylvania

Assistant Field Director, 1960 - 1966

Promoted, organized, and implemented volunteer activities on military installation and within military community. Provided personal and family counseling services, coordinated financial assistance, and furnished information regarding government benefits and application procedures. Managed a staff of 100-300 volunteers.

EDUCATION

Bachelor of Philosophy, University of Maryland, College Park, Maryland, 1960

Professional Training
Numerous seminars and courses in Criminal Investigations and Immigration Officers Training
15 credits toward a Master of Arts in Administration of Justice

AWARDS

- Letters of commendation from two Assistant United States Attorneys for performance as case agent in two cases, 1990 and 1991.

- Excellent performance rating, 1985 and 1986.

- Letter of Commendation from Assistant Attorney General, July 28, 1981.

- Outstanding Performance of Duty, July 1975.

- Sustained Superior Performance of Duty, July 1974.

- Quality increase, 1970.

HARRIS W. CASEWELL

33 King Street, Alexandria, Virginia 22310 (703) 555-XXXX

CAREER OBJECTIVE: A position as a Statistician in either a research or applied environment.

BACKGROUND SUMMARY

Strong analytical and computational skills. Expertise in analyzing and summarizing complex survey data and presenting results to technical and non-technical audiences.

EXPERIENCE

Applied Research, Inc., Washington, D.C.

STATISTICIAN, Advanced Analysis Practice, 1992 - present

Apply multivariate statistical methods in the development of customer satisfaction models for a national governmental household survey. Prepare sampling specifications and instruct subcontractor in the implementation of customized multiple comparison tests into final reports.

> Develop marketing segmentation models using cluster analysis and canonical discriminant analysis enabling clients to determine behavioral profiles of their target populations.

> Utilize categorical data analysis procedures such as loglinear modeling, logistic regression, and multidimensional preference analysis to explain relationships among and between variables for both industry and government survey data, with emphasis on service quality studies.

Department of Defense, Washington, D.C.

QUALITY ASSURANCE SPECIALIST, Publications Division, 1987 - 1992

Contracting Officer's Technical Representative (COTR) for publication division's production and inventory management and control system. System enabled real-time job tracking and scheduling of all agency printing. Developed and implemented an interim job tracking and reporting system on a microcomputer network. Top Secret Security Clearance.

> Set up an internal measurement system to measure and control errors pertaining to printing production quality. Applied statistical quality control procedures resulting in improved product and process quality.

> Designed experiments and performed Analysis of Variance (ANOVA) hypothesis testing on complex printing/imaging problems to isolate causes of variability. Determined confidence intervals for system capabilities.

> Devised automated estimating procedures for printing jobs through the application of multiple regression models.

> Established automated monthly statistical reports for detecting trends pertaining to errors in the publishing/printing process.

> Created and ran computer simulation model to determine optimum scheduling system for classified waste disposal system.

U. S. Government Printing Office, Washington, D.C.

PHOTOGRAPHIC TECHNOLOGIST, Quality Control Department, 1979 - 1987

Developed and implemented comprehensive microfiche quality assurance program which included: attributes to be measured, tolerances for defect classification, and statistical sampling plans. Incorporated this program into contractual document for procurement of microfiche by all government agencies.

Directed production studies to establish reliable and measurable process performance criteria such as dot reproduction capabilities of contact papers and duplication of films.

COMPUTER SKILLS

SAS (on mainframes in CMS, VAX/VMS, and MVS environments and PCs), SPSS, BMDP, Lotus 1-2-3, FORTRAN, IMSL, dBase III+ (network as well as single user), GPSS, Pascal, Minitab, SuperCalc, Harvard Graphics, WordPerfect, WordStar, EXP, LINDO.

EDUCATION

George Mason University, Fairfax, Virginia
M.S., Statistics, 1992

Specializations: Multivariate Statistics, Categorical Data Analysis, Multiple Regression, Robust and Exploratory Data Analysis, and Simulation.

Master's Thesis: *Robust Estimation of Canonical Correlation.*

Rochester Institute of Technology, Rochester, New York
B.S., Imaging Science, 1979

PROFESSIONAL ORGANIZATIONS

American Statistical Association
Washington Statistical Society
American Society for Quality Control

MARY HADDON LAMB

8332 Common Street, Menlo Park, California 94025

Work (415) 777-XXXX   Home (415) 999-XXXX

CAREER HISTORY

More than 22 years of **systems engineering** and **program management** experience. Managed major Federal Government contracts for the past 12 years.

Selected Accomplishments

- Systems Manager and Group Manager for large-scale system development efforts involving eight clients in a facilities management environment.

- Prime contractor and manager for project involving data center construction, ADP and telecommunications hardware acquisition and installation, network configuration and implementation, application software design, user training, hardware maintenance, and facilities management for Middle Eastern country, Ministry of Defense.

- Managed significant elements of a major proposal effort resulting in the largest ADP systems integration project in Government being awarded by the Air Force.

- Managed the design, development, and implementation of an on-line interactive financial and accounting control system for federal agency.

- Program Manager for ADP hardware deployment, process control, software design, development, and implementation at 350 facilities throughout the United States.

- Developed fee-for-service methodologies used in commercial and government environments and led more than 200 professionals involved in more than 32 simultaneous and independent projects.

- Established integrated client/server, LAN-based, and CASE tool systems engineering environments for all phases of company's systems life cycle.

- Led the migration of government communications system from a mainframe environment to a distributed client/server environment.

WORK HISTORY

NATIONAL TELECOMMUNICATIONS, INC.

       Program Manager, Menlo Park, California, 1991 - present
       Project Manager, Washington, D.C., 1988 - 1991
       Regional Manager, Phoenix, Arizona, 1983 - 1987
       Area Manager, Menlo Park, California, 1979 - 1982
       Project Director, Menlo Park, California, 1970 - 1978

U.S. NAVY, FIELD OPERATIONS

       Program Officer, Washington, D.C., 1964 - 1970

EDUCATION

M.S., Management Science, University of California, Riverside, Riverside, California
B.S., Marine Engineering, California Polytechnic State University, San Luis Obispo, California

SHIRLEY B. HALL
988 Evans Street
San Diego, California 92196
(619) 888-XXXX

**An elementary education professional with excellent communication skills
and expertise in language arts and reading.**

EXPERIENCE

READING TEACHER

Amelia Heights Elementary School, San Diego, California, 1991 - present

- Test and diagnose high-risk, multicultural students in reading.

- Create individualized reading and writing programs to meet student needs. Conduct workshops for parents and participate in evaluating and recommending services for children with learning and emotional problems.

ELEMENTARY SCHOOL TEACHER

Amelia Heights Elementary School, San Diego, California, 1989 - 1991
Blake Lane Elementary School, Los Angeles, California, 1986 - 1989
Shady Brook Elementary School, Los Altos, California, 1976 - 1979

- Taught grades 1 - 4. Implemented a writing program and developed an incentive reading program that improved student reading skills.

- Worked closely with L.D. and Reading teachers to address special needs.

- Piloted a Language Experience Approach to Reading program.

- Created a newsletter to communicate with parents.

SUBSTITUTE TEACHER

Redwood Elementary School, San Francisco, California, 1984 - 1985
Green Lake Elementary School, Los Altos, California, 1981 - 1983

- Taught English, Language Arts, Science, and History to grades 1 - 4 in teachers' absence.

EDUCATION

M.ED., Reading, San Diego State University, San Diego, California, 1990

B.A., Elementary Education, University of California, Davis, Davis, California, 1976

CERTIFICATION

Elementary Grades K - 6, Permanent, State of California

MEREDITH CAPLAN

Present Address
55 High Street
Newark, Delaware
(302)222-XXXX

Permanent Address
6 South Street
Baltimore, Maryland 21200
(301)444-XXXX

OBJECTIVE

A position as a Marketing Education Teacher in a secondary school.

EDUCATION

B.S. in Marketing Education, 1993, Dean's List, GPA 3.5
Provisional Certificate K - 12
DELAWARE VALLEY COLLEGE, Dover, Delaware

TEACHING EXPERIENCE

Student Teacher, Williams High School, Wilmington, Delaware, 1992 - 1993

Assumed full responsibility for teaching marketing to grades 9 and 10 for 8 weeks. Planned, organized, and executed lesson plans. Attended staff development workshops for high school teachers. Participated in parent-teacher meetings at the end of the grading period.

MARKETING EXPERIENCE

Sales Assistant, Elegance, Wilmington, Delaware, Summers 1989 - 1992

Assisted customers, arranged merchandise, restocked shelves, and handled cash and sales transactions. Communicated special requests and trends to management. Took inventory and set up displays.

Sales Assistant, Victoria's Secret, Baltimore, Maryland, Summer 1988

Performed a wide range of sales duties for specialty lingerie retail operation. Created effective window and in-store displays. Assisted customers in selecting and sizing merchandise. Handled sales transactions.

SKILLS

Moderately fluent in Spanish and French; Proficient with IBM PC and WordPerfect.

COLLEGE ACTIVITIES

Student Ambassador: Selected to represent school at official functions, directed tours of the university for potential students and their families, and assisted in coordinating the annual university phon-a-thon.

Panhellenic Executive Council: Headed scholarship banquets and activities; interviewed, selected, trained, and directed 70 Rush counselors for 600 Rushees.

```
┌─────────┐
│ Résumé  │
│   93    │
└─────────┘
```

MARY ELINOR WHITE
7554 East Avenue, Rochester, New York 14617
(716) 777-XXXX

CAREER SUMMARY

Eight years of experience teaching Mathematics and Computer Science; five years of experience creating the master schedules and assigning students to classes.

COURSES TAUGHT

Algebra I	Algebra II/Trigonometry
Algebra I/II	Geometry
Algebra II	Freshman Word Processing
Trigonometry/Analytic Geometry	AP Computer Science - Levels A and AB
Computer Literacy	Word processing, databases, speadsheets

EMPLOYMENT HISTORY

Teacher, Mathematics, Monroe Academy, Rochester, New York, 1985 - present

Substitute Teacher, 7th and 8th Grade Algebra, Erie County Public Schools, Buffalo, New York, 1982 - 1984

Teacher, Mathematics, Monroe County Public Schools, Rochester, New York, 1972 - 1980

EDUCATION

M.A. in Education, Hamilton College, Clinton, New York, 1972

B.A. in Economics, Cornell University, Ithaca, New York, 1970
  Honors: Honorary Prize Scholar, Dean's List, 1967 - 1970

CERTIFICATION

A Collegiate Professional Certificate, Mathematics, New York State

PROFESSIONAL DEVELOPMENT

"Analytic Geometry and Calculus I and II," University of Rochester, 1990 - 1991

"Summer Math for Teachers," University of Rochester, 1989

"Computers in the Mathematics Curriculum," National Council of Teachers of Mathematics, 1986

Math Center Methods Seminar, The Math Center, Washington, D.C., 1985

PROFESSIONAL ASSOCIATIONS

National Council of Teachers of Mathematics

OPHELIA DALTON
4 Rocky Road, Eugene, Oregon 97403
(503) 788-XXXX

CAREER HISTORY

Seventeen years in the field of education with an expertise in devising strategies for students with specific learning needs. Experienced in developing, implementing, and training staff in the use of specialized curricula for varied populations.

EXPERIENCE

SPECIAL EDUCATION TEACHER

The Patterson Children Home, Eugene, Oregon   1992 - present

Teacher for children who are emotionally handicapped. Generate individual educational plans and testing modifications. Instruct in all subject areas, modify curriculum, and manage classroom.

PROJECT COORDINATOR

State Health Education Center, Salem, Oregon   1990 - 1991

Coordinated project and developed Resource Guide for *Lion's Journey*, a substance abuse prevention program to be used with students who are emotionally handicapped, grades K - 8. Developed and published an HIV/AIDS risk-reduction program for youth at-risk. Implemented and trained staff in use of the program curriculum, including peer leadership training and parent education. Planned and implemented health-related training programs. Evaluated materials for professional library. Conducted project research and evaluation activities.

PROGRAM RESOURCE SPECIALIST

The Adult Center, Salem, Oregon   1981 - 1990

Created, implemented, and instructed staff in use of specialized curriculum. Trained adults with developmental disabilities in academic and social skills. Set up and implemented community education program and internal program evaluation system. Initiated and supervised student internship with local colleges and volunteer programs. Established agency systems to ensure compliance with state regulations for day treatment programs servicing individuals with developmental disabilities. Conducted inservice training programs. Wrote and presented grant proposals. Developed format and wrote agency Policy and Procedure Manual.

RESOURCE ROOM TEACHER

Beaverton Central School, Beaverton, Oregon   1980 - 1981

Defined program goals and recommended instruction modifications for students in mainstreamed classes. Diagnosed and planned strategies for remediation of specific learning deficits. Prepared students for Competency Tests in reading, writing, and mathematics.

SPECIAL TEACHING ASSIGNMENT

Beaverton Central School, Beaverton, Oregon   1980 - 1981

Teacher for home-bound child with developmental disabilities. Established program of instruction and home management.

CERTIFICATION

Permanent, State of Oregon for grades Nursery - 6 and Special Classes of the Mentally Retarded

EDUCATION

Master of Science, Education, University of Oregon, Eugene, Oregon
Bachelor of Science, Education and Behavioral Science, Oregon State University, Corvallis, Oregon
   Magna cum laude
   Dean's List
   Behavioral Science Honors
Certificate, National Council on Alcoholism and Other Drug Addictions, Eugene, Oregon

PUBLICATIONS

Involving Youth in HIV Education: An Interactive Approach, Regional Health Education Center, Salem, Oregon

Co-author, *Healthy Habits* (Grade 2), Educational Publishers, Eugene, Oregon

Contributing author, *Curriculum Resource Manual*, Crater Educational Publishers, New York, New York

Co-author and contributor to seven functional activity guides, *Senior Strategies*, The Adult Center, Salem, Oregon

PROFESSIONAL AFFILIATIONS

Board Member, Eugene Coordinating Council for People With Disabilities

Past Member, State of Oregon Professional Health Educator's Conference Planning Committee

```
┌─────────┐
│ Résumé  │
│   95    │
└─────────┘
```

THOMAS K. ROSSINI

1522 Tenth Avenue, Baltimore, Maryland 21233
(410) 828-XXXX

CAREER SUMMARY

Extensive data communications experience at AT&T with a technical expertise. A team player, bottom line-oriented, who gets the job done.

- Excellent interpersonal skills and the ability to work effectively with all staff levels, inside and outside the organization.
- Strong writing and organizational skills.

PROFESSIONAL EXPERIENCE AND ACCOMPLISHMENTS

Data Communications/Technical

- Provided support coverage for computer room operations personnel. Maintained Wang, Penta, Data General, Infotron, and Octel hardware and software.
- Installed, maintained, tested, analyzed, and serviced key telephones, data communications, and a variety of terminal equipment including Teletype, D.E.C., Data General, Aspen Voice Mail, and personal computers for major corporate accounts, government agencies, and AT&T.
- Provided support to Director, Building Operations, and Engineering for Capital and Expense budget. Trained in MR/IBPS and FCS to collect and analyze financial data for district.
- Negotiated design of systems (communications, electrical, vertical transportation, HVAC, etc.) for Two AT&T Plaza.

Customer Support

- Executed orders from inception to completion for the Wang Office Automation Systems and Penta Electronic Publishing at One AT&T Plaza and implemented orders for Data General Advanced Office System, regionwide, and the Octel Voice Mail systems for N.S.I. locations.
- Launched District Quality Improvement Team and served as Administrator.
- Initiated "Brown Bag" informational lunches for One AT&T Plaza.
- Met with senior management and consultants and presented alternatives for Two AT&T Plaza project.

Management

- Managed operations at One AT&T Plaza. Supervised five mechanics and one clerk.
- Directed contract guard service, house service, plant maintenance, elevator maintenance, electricians, and other contract labor.
- Saved over $100,000 in one year by implementing many Best Cost measures and reducing expenses at AT&T Plaza.
- Initiated paper, cardboard, and aluminum recycling for location.
- Collaborated on Best Cost Solutions week at AT&T Plaza.

RELEVANT SKILLS

Writing
- Organized project and prepared user guidelines for external affairs clients on Wang system.
- Wrote monthly informational bulletins for building tenants.
- Abstracted and summarized proposals for new building construction.

Computer
- PC Literate: WordPerfect, Lotus 1-2-3, Communication Software - Crosstalk, Procomm.
- Knowledge of AT&T Computer Systems: Data General, Wang, Uniplex, PC LAN.

EMPLOYMENT HISTORY

AT&T, 1978 - present

Assistant Manager, 1991 - present
Budgets and District Support, Real Estate

Assistant Manager, 1990 - 1991
Property Management, Real Estate

Assistant Manager, 1989 - 1990
Real Estate Facilities, Real Estate

Assistant Staff Manager, 1987 - 1989
Office Automation Implementation, Support Services

Field Operations, 1978 - 1987
Data Communications Provisioning, Operations

EDUCATION

Bachelor of Arts, 1978
University of Maryland, College Park, Maryland

Professional Development
Numerous courses in technical and management development

DENISE MOSS

922 Farm Hill Road, Charleston, West Virginia 25304
(304) 888-XXXX

CAREER SUMMARY

Extensive experience as an electronics and computer technician. Component level repair, configuration and quality control testing of IBM and IBM compatible PC, XT, AT, 80386 and 80486 computers and peripherals.

EXPERIENCE

COMPUTER CORPORATION OF AMERICA, Charleston, West Virginia, 1989 - present
TECHNICAL SERVICE MANAGER, 1992 - present

Promoted to manager providing technical service support to government and commercial customers, ensuring equipment and customer satisfaction. Utilize technical expertise to repair personal computers, solve customer configuration, and operation inquiries/problems. Perform on-site servicing. Oversee shipping and receiving and inventory control. Prepare monthly reports.

COMPUTER TECHNICIAN, 1990 - 1992

Assembled, configured, and conducted quality control testing of IBM and compatible computers and peripherals to end user specifications. Repaired and upgraded third-party computers and peripherals to customer specifications.

ASSEMBLY TECHNICIAN, 1989 - 1990

Assembled and tested IBM PS/2 computers for state government contract. Repaired TEMPEST modified computers and peripherals to component level. Received **Excellence in Service** award.

APPLIANCE REPAIRS, INC., Columbus, Ohio, 1988 - 1989
TELEVISION TECHNICIAN, 1988 - 1989

Repaired and maintained name brand televisions including Sharp, RCA, Zenith, Magnavox, and Toshiba.

MONTGOMERY WARD, Columbus, Ohio, 1980 - 1988
SERVICE TECHNICIAN, 1986 - 1988

Promoted to service department repairing and maintaining equipment including TV's, VCR's, audio components, and garage door openers. As night shift supervisor, handled call assignments, dispatched field service technicians, serviced carry-in repairs. Secured and closed shop.

CREDIT CLERK, 1980 - 1986

Performed data entry for credit profiles. Resolved or forwarded customer inquiries. Researched credit history for approval/denial of credit and notified applicants of credit status.

EDUCATION

Associate in Specialized Technology, Electronics Technology, 1983
Cleveland Institute of Electronics, Cleveland, Ohio

Technical Training
Columbus State Community College, Columbus, Ohio, **VCR Repair Course**, 1989
Mitsubishi Electric Sales of America, Cypress, California, **VCR Troubleshooting Course**, 1988
Montgomery Ward Technical Training Center, Wheeling, West Virginia, **VCR Quick Service**, 1988
Montgomery Ward Technical Training Center, Wheeling, West Virginia, **Practical Color TV Servicing**, 1987
Montgomery Ward Extension Institute, Newark, Ohio, **Digital Technology - Microcomputers,** 1984 - 1985

MATHEW KELLEY
1335 Park Street, St. Paul, Minnesota 55108
Work (612) 622-XXXX Home (612) 623-XXXX

BACKGROUND SUMMARY

Extensive progressive telecommunications experience with an emphasis on large cable designs. Technical expertise and the ability to solve problems with innovative solutions.

EXPERIENCE

AMERICAN SYSTEMS INC., 1967 - present

Assistant Project Supervisor, St. Paul, Minnesota, 1990 - present

Supervise subcontract cable projects from 100 to 3,000 lines. Estimate materail costs and provide building, plant, and campus cable engineering, layout, and provisioning.

Ensured established quality procedures were followed and projects completed on time and within budget.

Produced quick and accurate engineering and cost estimates at less than 1% installed cost variance.

Contributed to customer satisfaction and quality reputation by eliminating hidden costs and effectively meeting customer requirements.

Installation/Maintenance Supervisor, Minneapolis, Minnesota, 1986 - 1990

Supervised staff of five to nine technicians in installation of large PABX switches. Motivated and trained staff, consistently bringing projects in at targeted margin.

Site Survey Engineer, St. Paul, Minnesota, 1980 - 1986

Shared in successful marketing effort; maintained best cost, developed effective wiring designs; created presentations and easily communicated wiring plans to customers.

Installation/Maintenance Technician, Minneapolis, Minnesota, 1973 - 1980

Installed and maintained large key systems in office buildings.

Central Office Repairman, Minneapolis, Minnesota, 1967 - 1973

Repaired central office switching equipment.

PROFESSIONAL TRAINING

Extensive training in telecommunications hardware and plant installation.

LOIS FISHER

4 Dogwood Drive, Chapel Hill, North Carolina
(919) 555-XXXX (Work) (919) 455-XXXX (Home)

Extensive experience as a trainer, manager, and writer with expertise in the fields of management and career development. Excellent oral and written communication skills. Author of two career books.

WORK HISTORY

APPLIED MANAGEMENT, INC.

SENIOR TRAINER, 1991 - present

Develop and conduct training programs on management, career, and professional development topics that improve communications and foster teamwork, increasing productivity and job satisfaction. Design curriculum; create and produce materials, handbooks, and workbooks.

CITY OF CHAPEL HILL

CAREER PLANNING PROGRAM SPECIALIST, 1980 - 1990
INSTRUCTOR, 1979 - 1990

Administered career and life planning program for largest school district in North Carolina. Developed and coordinated courses. Recruited, interviewed, hired, and supervised 25 - 30 instructors. Taught numerous workshops in career planning and changing, professional development, and job search skills.

Experienced 110% growth in student enrollment. Increased course offerings by 70%. Designed a career counseling program, developed alternative career work styles, career explorations, and job hunting preparation. Created programs with local high technology and health care industries, offering career exploration at the work site.

KATHARINE GIBBS SCHOOL

INSTRUCTOR, 1977 - 1978

Taught classes in "Introduction to Management," "Supervisory Management," "Effective Business Writing," and "Professionalism at Work."

XEROX CORPORATION

DISTRICT BILLING MANAGER, 1975 - 1977
OFFICE SERVICES SUPERVISOR, 1974 - 1975
CUSTOMER SERVICE MANAGER, 1971 - 1974
ADMINISTRATION, 1970 - 1971

Direct responsibility for staffs of 7 to 22; recruited, supervised, developed position descriptions; created and utilized training material; established performance criteria and appraised performance.

Successfully and consistently exceeded corporate performance targets in billing and credit and collections. Managed billing department for machine population of 16,000 units and annual revenue of $66 million.

Administered a new major account price plan for 25 accounts. Developed and presented a training program on complex contractual terms for senior-level customers, sales staff, and administrative personnel.

Supervised administrative secretarial communication network for 22 secretaries supporting 200 managers. Conducted awareness seminars, teambuilding workshops, and third-party counseling.

EDUCATION

Bachelor of Arts in English, 1981
   University of North Carolina, Chapel Hill, North Carolina

Xerox Corporation Management Training
   Management Studies, New Manager Seminar, Managing for Motivation, Management Action Workshop

PROFESSIONAL DEVELOPMENT

Strong Training Program, Qualifying Workshop, Consulting Psychologists Press (CPP), 1991

Myers-Briggs Type Indicator (*MBTI*), TYPEWATCHING Qualifying Workshop, Otto Kroeger Associates, 1989

PUBLICATIONS

BOOKS

Craft Your Career, ABC Books, New York, New York, 1990

Corporate Career Management, ABC Books, New York, New York, 1988

ARTICLES

"Career Planning Tips," American Executive, July/August 1991

"Career Tips," monthly career column, Magnolia Publications, January 1988 - November 1990

"Resume Writing Tips and Traps," *IIA Today*, March/April 1989

"A 12-Step Approach To Career Success," *The Woman Engineer*, Fall 1988

PROFESSIONAL ASSOCIATIONS

American Society for Training and Development (ASTD)
Association for Psychological Type (APT)

151

ALEXANDER W. IVES

8 Granite Lane, Denver, Colorado 80217
Work (303) 888-XXXX Home (303) 777-XXXX

CAREER HISTORY

A dedicated leader with progressive experience in the training department of a major information technology firm. A seasoned manager with strong organizational, analytical, and problem-solving skills interacting and communicating effectively with all organizational levels.

EXPERTISE IN:

- Curriculum design and delivery of management and career development training.
- Executive development selection and training.
- Total quality management system implementation.
- Organizational needs analysis and developmental planning.
- Measurement and evaluation of program effectiveness.

WORK HISTORY

INFORMATION TECHNOLOGY INC., Denver, Colorado

Regional Manager, Leadership Development   1991 - present

Manage a staff of 18 in the delivery and design of leadership and career development curriculum, and effectively meet the needs of all management levels and individual employees. Consult with business units to identify needs, develop training plans, and revise curriculum. Measure training program effectiveness and employee achievement. Act as informational resource for education technology. Frequent speaker and lecturer at customer functions.

- Exceeded all instructional productivity and student goals with budget savings of 8%, $250,000 less than 2 comparable training centers.
- Obtained highest rating of all training centers in the annual quality reviews. Customer component indicated complete satisfaction in curriculum, delivery and development, customer support, and overall service.

Manager, Leadership Development   1988 - 1991

Direct responsibility for staff of 9. Managed instructor development, course and seminar design, and customer marketing efforts. Supervised training administration, scheduling, and student recordkeeping. Managed $800,000 budget. Created job aids to guide managers in developing their staffs. Initiated the design of alternate training means, notably computer-based training and self-instructional texts. Planned regional conferences and customized workshops to reduce costs and improve training efficiency.

- Tripled productivity with only a one-third increase in staff. Reduced the training cost per student for three consecutive years.

Instructor, Leadership Development   1986 - 1988

Conducted training programs on management and career development topics. Designed and enhanced curriculum and created and produced training activities, materials, and workbooks. Accelerated employee development by implementing adjunct instructor program.

- Rated in top 10% of instructor group with student approval ratings of 91 - 98%. Doubled the region's customer base through the use of Mobile Training Teams.
- Authored principal guide for people development, *Leadership 2000*, which received corporate-wide acclaim. Contributed articles to corporate publications on management initiatives.

Deputy and Director Human Resources Division, HQMC   1983 - 1986

Managed second largest division within a Human Resources Department, acting as the proponent for quality of life projects. Directed personnel support and assistance programs during extensive growth.

- Increased productivity and decreased personnel requirement by 15% by initiating policies and introducing automated procedures. Successfully implemented a theme of quality customer service.

Chief of Staff, Marine Division, Okinawa, Japan   1982 - 1983

Reported to the top executive and directed the administration and operation of seven departments. Developed policy supporting hierarchy objectives. Provided daily policy interpretation, analyses, and recommendations.

- Effectively assumed executive responsibilities for a staff of 120 in chief executive's absence. Participated in major exercises in 2 foreign nations as an emergency stand-in; successfully demonstrated the ability to conduct a multinational amphibious operation.

Director, Career Planning Branch, HQMC   1979 - 1982

Managed service-wide programs for employee retention and management counseling. Developed program policy, procedures, and standards.

- Dramatically improved employee retention; designed new incentives and enhanced field operative training. Filled Marine Corps need for critical skills by instituting a variable bonus program.

Commanding Officer, Headquarters Battalion   1977 - 1979

Overall responsibility for unit of 1,200 including morale and personal well-being. Directed staff and unit leadership in administration, operations, and training.

- Reduced involuntary turnover rate 50% and tripled retention rate. Evaluated as #1 of 6 in annual performance and review.

Director, Strategy Department, Marine War College   1975 - 1977

Supervised the development and delivery of 15% of the college's curriculum for mid-level managers. Doubled the learning retention of class material through the introduction of new delivery modes such as simulation and case studies.

- Developed a Global Strategy course that 95% of the students opted to take as their elective.

EDUCATION

Graduate Studies, National University of Buenos Aires, Argentina, as a George Olmsted Scholar
Masters of Science in International Relations, University of Colorado at Denver, Denver, Colorado
Bachelor of Science in Engineering, U.S. Naval Academy, Annapolis, Maryland

PROFESSIONAL ASSOCIATIONS

Society for Human Resources Management
American Society for Training and Development

SOL SANDS

8 Sandstone Court, Phoenix, Arizona 85060
(602) 393-XXXX

QUALIFICATION SUMMARY

Progressive experience in the travel industry. Strong technical skills with a thorough working knowledge of airline and computer systems.

Fluent in French and Spanish and working knowledge of Italian and Portuguese.

EXPERIENCE

TRAVEL AGENT
Worldwide Travel, Inc., Phoenix, Arizona, 1992 - 1993

Promoted and assumed increased responsibility handling international computer reservations and itineraries. Managed ten major corporate accounts. Developed expertise with the Sabre Computer System. Quality control office specialist.

TRAVEL CONSULTANT
Travel American, Phoenix, Arizona, 1990 - 1992

Handled commercial/corporation accounts, leisure/vacation travel, and international and domestic ticketing reservations. Worked with small groups and cruises, making hotel and car arrangements.

TRAVEL AGENT
Worldwide Travel, Tuscon, Arizona, 1989 - 1990

Assisted commercial and retail accounts with domestic/international ticketing and reservations, package and individual tours, and cruises. Made rail, hotel, and car arrangements.

EDUCATION

A. A. S. in Travel and Tourism, Arizona Western College, Yuma, Arizona, 1989

TRAVEL

Great Britain	Luxembourg	Philippines	Switzerland
Portugal	France	Greece	Turkey
Italy	China	Thailand	Hong Kong
Germany	Canada	Spain	Guatemala
Bermuda	Mexico	the Caribbean	

ROBYN M. IRVING
7665 Sahara Street
Las Vegas, Nevada 99100
Work (702) 777-XXXX Home (702) 333-XXXX

QUALIFICATIONS SUMMARY

Capable office administrator with excellent administrative and supervisory skills. Interact extensively and effectively with all staff levels and individuals with diverse backgrounds.

EXPERIENCE

WORD PROCESSING ADMINISTRATOR
GOLDEN CASINO AND HOTEL, Las Vegas, Nevada, 1989 - present

Supervise word processing production center for casino and hotel with 420 employees. Process all performance appraisals, company directory, reports, and correspondence. Prioritize production and supervise typing. Manage a staff of four.

Establish office systems and maintain information storage and processing. Select and install personal computers and software. Utilize WordPerfect, Microsoft Word, and Lotus 1-2-3.

Create and conduct training programs on software applications and office administration.

OFFICE ADMINISTRATOR
HKL CONSTRUCTION, INC., Las Vegas, Nevada, 1982 - 1989

Provided administrative support to President and executive staff of commercial construction company. Maintained calendars; prepared confidential reports; composed and typed correspondence. Scheduled travel and meetings. Created filing systems.

Managed word processing systems. Installed and maintained computer hardware and software. Developed office procedures and acted as office computer expert.

WORD PROCESSING SPECIALIST
EAGLE SPORTSWEAR, Los Angeles, California, 1978 - 1982

Organized and processed written and dictated materials for 100 users in 12 departments. Developed excellent editing and proofreading skills. Conducted training on word processing equipment. Prepared statistical and audit reports, procedure manuals, and handbooks.

TRAINING

PROFESSIONAL DEVELOPMENT
175 Continuing Education Units (CEU) in office administration and management.
TECHNICAL TRAINING
Proficient with IBM PC and Macintosh. Numerous courses in computer and software applications. Adept at using word processing, desktop publishing, and spreadsheet programs.